Blind Vision
VOLUME III

I0099928

VALOR
IN
PROSPERITY

CURTIS C. GRECO

Advantage®

Published by Advantage, Charleston, South Carolina.
Member of Advantage Media Group.

ADVANTAGE is a registered trademark and the Advantage colophon is a trademark of Advantage Media Group, Inc.

Printed in the United States of America.

ISBN: 978-1-59932-171-4
LCCN: 2010908438

Most Advantage Media Group titles are available at special quantity discounts for bulk purchases for sales promotions, premiums, fundraising, and educational use. Special versions or book excerpts can also be created to fit specific needs.

For more information, please write: Special Markets, Advantage Media Group, P.O. Box 272, Charleston, SC 29402 or call 1.866.775.1696.

Visit us online at **advantagefamily**.com

"The American Government needs to play guard for its people. Curtis Greco's third book in the Blind Vision Series, Valor in Prosperity, calls for new leadership and new rules of conduct on the court and in the field. If the thoughts shapers and citizens of this country were to heed the advice herein, we would all be blessed with the Championship Title."

—PAT WILLIAMS, SENIOR VICE PRESIDENT, ORLANDO MAGIC, AUTHOR OF *NAIL IT!* & *DALY WISDOM*

"Curtis Greco has done it again. The third installment in The Blind Vision Series provides visionary solutions for the daunting challenges our nation is now facing. Americans need to join the conversation now to propagate badly needed, swift reforms."

—AUSTIN HILL, COLUMNIST, TALK SHOW HOST, AUTHOR OF *THE VIRTUES OF CAPITALISM: A MORAL CASE FOR FREE MARKETS*

"Valor in Prosperity *is a compelling call to action for the American people to stand up and reclaim their country. This third book in Curtis Greco's important series presents the exclamation point to his overall message, The Functional Stimulus. Finally, a series of workable solutions to the problems that plague us all.*"

—TODD ZAUGG, PRINCIPAL & FOUNDER, MATRIX ACHIEVEMENT GROUP, LLC, AUTHOR, *WARRIOR SALES MONK*

DEDICATION

"...we mutually pledge to each other our Lives,
our Fortunes, and our sacred Honor."

To Vincent and Claire, the image of what's possible!

To Americans the world over! This Series is my Gift to you!

But most of all,

To an Infinite and Perfect Love, binding one and all, from whom
"meaning and form" finds its cause!

Blind Vision

NOT SO LONG AGO I had the occasion to sit and visit with my father. At that time, he had progressed well into his 80's and though time had waged a battle with his body, his mind was as crisp as ever. I asked his opinion about the times we are living in and what he observed, over the years, to be the most significant changes. I was amazed by what he said.

- "People, at their core, never really change. However, I have noticed that we seem to have moved away from them [core values]."

- "Despite what history may say, people were not happy about what Roosevelt was doing…it's not all that different from what I see happening today."

- "If there had been the same media exposure of global affairs in the 30's and 40's, Pearl Harbor would never have happened and the American people would have felt much different about the war and Roosevelt would never have been elected."

- "This technology thing – yes, information is more easily obtained, but I think it has pushed people into being more detached and ambivalent."

- "But the thing I've noticed most is that people seem to have lost their sense of common purpose."

If I were to add anything to his comments, I would say the abstract notion of consequence has been degraded and seems to be fading on toward oblivion. We have become desensitized not only to the impact our choices have on our own lives, but perhaps equally important, the impact our choices have on others. This series takes an overview of fiscal interests and policy, not only of the United States, but also of the world, and further examines the financial and social consequences of those very policies. However, I believe the most critical perspective from which to view these issues is through the lens of freedom and the definitive critique of what constitutes the expressions of, or impediments to, liberty.

In one sense, the series may be seen as a *call to action*, in another respect, it may be viewed as a "political and economic retrospective." At best, it may even be both.

To illustrate and underscore this body of work and my own observations and conclusions, I have drawn on a few of my favorite historical figures, such as Thomas Jefferson, Benjamin Franklin, Andrew Jackson, and Don Miguel de Cervantes, to name a few.

A final note on the series title, *Blind Vision*. I appreciate the use of words, in combination, to paint a mental picture from which to convey a message. Let me explain further: Many years ago, I lost an older sister to a congenital heart disorder. Today, modern medicine would likely have saved her; however, it was a different time. Her name was Cynthia – to me though, she was simply known as Cindy. In addition to her heart condition, she was also blind, though she had so well adapted, one would never have known.

As one of 10 children, I am positioned in the younger half of the regiment and occasionally Cindy would be assigned the task of minding a few of the younger group. I was always amazed, no, I was stunned by how she managed to know what sort of trouble I was brewing and her proficiency in interfering with most of my misadventures. I can still, to this very day, clearly hear her voice: "Curtis!"

I recall asking her, "How do you do it?" and she replied, "I'm blind, but I can still see what I know!" Many years would pass and this moment, like others before or since, resolved to memory storage until June of 2008. I had just concluded a talk with a group. A few folks approached me and we began a spirited exchange. As I recall it, I found myself responding to one of the questions with something like this: "Look, even if you were blind, your mind's eye will image what you know to be true!" Instantly, I saw the face of my sister Cindy and I heard her voice once again.

The most compelling reason for this series is my personal love for the ideals that inspired the creation of this country's form of government: "Life, Liberty and the Pursuit of Happiness!" I believe that man's greatest and ultimate challenge is to perfect the means to void his divisive tendencies. Each is called to express ones own unique gift which, in the process of our expressing, defines ones very purpose. However, a gift, by its very nature, can only be expressed in the physical realm and with the rhythm of action, and so, express it we must!

This gift must and will only ever occur freely and with unfettered interchange accompanied by the reward which, I believe, will inevitably come when all engage in the same pursuit. We must move smartly to perfect these ideals and overcome all impediments to its accomplishment. One might even say it is our collective "calling." There is no other place to go; the time is now and the place is right where one finds him or herself to be!

Once I accepted the challenge of actually taking on the project, I found myself wondering if what you are about to read is necessarily new. The manner in which I present the message may be novel and you may even find my own personal comments poetically enticing. However, the fact of the matter is, no matter how well scripted the message may be, we truly do already know the "core values!" I believe God has planted these seeds of truths and they are forever resident in one's mind and soul. They are what you intuitively know to be true.

How then does the idea relate to this three-part series? A fair question. The most efficient way to explain it might best be in the form of an allegory. For instance: A man is walking down the street on his way to work. Summer, winter, rain, snow or shine, year after year, he walks the same course day after day. Some days he gives and some days he receives but always what he carries is a function of what he collects from one place or another. Even without speaking, you know what he does for a living, don't you? Yes, of course you do. The markings are in the images your mind forms from the verbal cues of this simple story. Yes indeed, he's a postman. Simple enough!

Yes, of course the confusion of the day is marked by many indicators of truth sandwiched between the clutter of newspaper articles, five-second sound-bites, talk radio, non-stop breaking news, well crafted speeches and emails. Yet despite the confusion of mixed messages, the markings of what is "true" is found in our conscience which surfaces to filter the input. What we discover from this filtering process is the dissonance between what we observe and what we know, intuitively, to be true. All one is left with is a discordant sense of disbelief which is most conspicuously identified when one finds him or herself uttering: "Who do they think they're kidding?" Well, *they* think it's you!

I, like many, find myself more and more disenfranchised from a political system that bears no resemblance to the promise of our national heritage. Our national sovereignty and economic future has been repackaged and out-sourced with the speed and efficiency of an IRS tax lien; entire industries have been relocated, leaving behind vacant warehouses, silent factories, idle resources of all types and worst of all, broken dreams.

In a country whose very identity rests upon the genius of an ideal that prior to its formation had never seen the light of day, seeing the promise of this land and the industry of so vibrant and genuine a people summarily laid to waste is, as it is for most, simply heart breaking! And then of course are our children, I think of my own and I ask myself: "How can we let this stand?" I hear others say, "What has happened?" I hear even more say, "Somebody's got to do something about this!" And when I hear this comment, I often think of the following story which I heard some years ago. Perhaps one day I'll share the story of how I came to hear it.

It's a story about a man who walks in to a church. You see, he's down on his luck; he's lost his business, he's lost his family and his view of the world is hopeless and in complete disarray. He walks up to the altar and stares squarely at the image upon the cross and with the strained voice of a person in emotional and physical pain he attempts to impale the image with his words. "Why? Why have you done this to me? Why have you let the world fall upon me this way? The world is in turmoil and you sit idly by and just let it happen! What kind of love is this you speak of? How can you speak to me of goodness when this is to be the world in which a man finds himself? Why, oh why, don't you do something?" His energy spent, the room's light gently softens and becomes suddenly still. And then, awakening the stillness of the moment is the warmth of a soft resonant voice and it speaks these simple words: "I did; I sent you."

I'll ask of you this: Please do remember, in particular, the last five words of the preceding paragraph. They are a foundation on which to build a remarkable life!

And so, there it is, the overall message. Read it, enjoy it and be inspired by its message.

BLIND VISION

"I'VE NO NEED FOR VISION TO SEE WHAT I KNOW TO BE TRUE."

CURTIS C. GRECO, JUNE 2009

Contents

A Note from the Author

NOT ENOUGH IS SAID about the critical moments in one's life. We conceal these for various reasons, but often it is more likely that we think, "Oh, we'll get around to it!" or, "Ah, well, I'd better keep it to myself, no one will believe it!" This, however, is not one of those instances! I deliberately intend for all who read these works to know of a specific critical moment and the gratitude I hold in my heart for those who are integral to it! First, the entire staff at Advantage Media Group, an extraordinary group of talented individuals whose assembly is a monument to the truly remarkable vision of Adam Witty, an extraordinary man!

Vision can only ever truly be inspiring if, as its architect, there is an individual capable of its mastery. In Volumes I, II, and III of the *Blind Vision* series I introduce The Imperfect Messenger Foundation and I fully intend for it to become an iconic resource through which I and others disseminate thought provoking work. And yes, the material you have in hand is indeed the product of my efforts. However, the form you will soon view received its first breath of life from the inspired vision of Denis Boyles, AMG's Senior Editor to whom I will be eternally grateful! Then of course there is the idea of mastery; an idea which is truly only ever known when evidenced by action: Editor Priscilla Turner is the archetypical form of this ideal and as the case with Denis Boyles, demonstrates it so lovingly through her guidance, precision and elegant refinements. From where I started, even I could never have imagined the result and I will look forward to working with both again and again!

To say that I have saved the "best for last" would not be fair to those I've mentioned thus far so perhaps it is more appropriate for me to express my intention this way: I've saved the most dear for last! Gregg Stebben is an exceptionally gifted gentleman, I've known him since I was 15 years old and though we both accompanied events and careers which lead us on separate paths for much of this time, a wondrous fate brought us back together. For this, I've only to express a hearty thanks to his marvelous brother, Marty. To the point: It is no overstatement to say that none of what is before you would appear the way it does were it not for Gregg. He possesses a unique self-effacing form of warmth and gentleness that is supremely magnetic. He is an accomplished writer and media presence and most importantly, he is truly a good man in every sense of the word. I do my best to express regard and admiration for him at every possible opportunity!

And so you ask: "What is the 'critical moment?'" Consider, if you will, thinking of life as a canvas upon which each of us records and expresses our own unique and individual gift in a color and by a stroke uniquely our own. Not one stroke may be omitted, not one expression missed or unrecorded – to do so would forever change the image and then for all time it would remain incomplete! For me, with reference to this endeavor, the "critical moment" is this: That at one moment in time, I should be so blessed to have such magnificent talent expressing their gift upon my canvas! To omit just one would have made the outcome something different, something less! They have given me an extraordinary gift, which I now present to you, the reader, and I do believe we owe each other our very best effort! I couldn't possibly imagine a more perfect way to paint a life in color!

Note: Throughout the "Blind-Vision" series, distinct insertions appear in two conspicuous visual formats whose purpose is to enhance the specific commentary where and when they appear. As to the source of these enhancements, those in italicized form are referenced parenthetically or by footnote therein, those which are not referenced so are the product of the Series Author, Curtis C. Greco.

A Perspective

As TIME GOES BY I increasingly find myself a keen observer of 21st century social issues and most conspicuously of the pathology which, to me, lies at the core of our sociological devolution. For some time I seemed to struggle for clarity, a specific and tactile sense of what lied within the haze of my thinking. Much of the time I had a sense that what I was searching for was indeed there — however uncertain as to what *it* was — though resolute in knowing that when I happened upon the source, it would be patently clear.

Well indeed, I did happen upon the source and I defined the notion in this way: *Selective-indifference.* This term is the companion of others I've coined over the years, such as *Flat-Earth Idolatry* and *Practical Detachment*, and whose purpose is to define the instances where callous hubris seeks to redefine and redefine yet again various principles in such a way as to render them each perpetually malleable and thus, ultimately, completely meaningless - which of course serves the user's purpose and ultimate ambition. In the end, conveniently enough, this resolves the issue full-circle to the point of origin: *Selective-indifference.*

The most conspicuous application of this term, being as a means to cue or otherwise condense the primary ethos that lies behind this series, which is, at least as I observe, the near-perpetual redefining and redefining yet again of what it means to be possessors of unalienable rights as defined by the *Declaration of Independence*. More specifically, what if any relationship there is to the principles identified and defined by this document as *unalienable* and the guardians of the U.S. Constitution's allegiance to their preservation.

Many Americans may find it a bit unnerving to discover that as a founding document, so-called legal scholars pay little, if any, deference to the *Declaration of Independence* and treat it merely as an *incidental list of grievances.* The single most important document ever to come out of the Americas and revered world-wide as the preeminent symbol of the American ideal of self-government (republicanism), *nothing more than an incidental list of grievances*! How *selectively-indifferent* can one conveniently be?

I, of course, have little regard for innovative notions such as these and none more so than in the case of *selective-indifference* to the *Declaration of Independence.* After all, lest we forget, it was only upon the signing of the *Declaration* that the sovereign status - of the individuals inhabiting the Colonies - was forever defined. Further, it was at this point and only from this solemn act that the ability of the now sovereign-American existed in sufficient form to enable the construct, which became the U.S. Constitution, to have meaning and purpose to wit that it could be ratified "by the consent of the governed" such that it became a binding social contract.

To the point I intend to make: The U.S. Constitution is a document that enumerates (only) those functions in which the government may engage and in so doing simultaneously defines all possible permutations not "specifically enumerated herein" as specific prohibitions. For this document to have any meaning as both protector of *individual freedoms* and *liberties* must there not be an over-riding regiment, a declaration if you will, that defines what in essence are the freedoms and liberties to which the Constitution owes its allegiance to protect? A precedence, a construct or higher authority over and above the behemoth that is intrusive government - which when applied - gives context such that prohibitions and abuses are identifiable and thus restrained?

Well, I'll simply submit to you, my readership, that if it is not the *Declaration of Independence* I scarcely know of what other possible medium the self-anointed legal scholars might have in mind; unless of course it is the supremely malleable interpretation-by-demand construct they deferentially refer to as *the law* and the process that orchestrates the same! If this is the case, there is no such thing as freedom and no such thing as liberty and man then is nothing more than chattel whose corporal form is forever left to the discretion of *the master* and *his* impulses. Where does this end? Ah yes, the state of *selective-indifference* to which I've previously referred.

> "TOLERANCE IS ONLY THE COERCIVE BRANDING REPRESENTING
> A FORCED ACCEPTANCE OF AN IRRECONCILABLE ACTION
> OR THOUGHT. IF THIS THEN IS THE CASE, INTOLERANCE
> CAN ONLY BE THE OPPOSING FORCE; THE PRESERVATION
> OF ONE'S SOUND ACTION OR THOUGHT."

With the previous series of paragraphs in mind, it should be easy to understand that in the absence of an acceptable code of conduct nearly any regiment of thought can be made to seem perfectly reasonable. By extending the command structure of *the law* to this now newly minted and perfectly reasonable interpretation we can see, as evidenced by the German Third Reich of the 1930's, you can make legal, or illegal for that matter, nearly anything ones mind can imagine! To my thinking, as I suspect to your own as well, this sounds like the ultimate playground bully having free reign! However, I am still of the opinion that:

"WE HAVE NOT YET PROGRESSED THROUGH NOR SUFFICIENTLY PERFECTED THE ART OF SELF-GOVERNMENT TO THE POINT WHERE WE HAVE AUTHORIZED MOVEMENT BEYOND ITS FRAMEWORK SUCH THAT WE CONCEDE TO ENFORCED COERCION OF THIS NATION AND ITS PEOPLE ON TOWARD THE VOID OF OBLIVION."

As a preamble to the last volume in the *Blind Vision Series,* it is vital to capture the essence of why *We Hold These Truths to be…* is, in both qualitative and quantitative form, so vital to your understanding of what the title of this last volume attempts to impart. Without the willingness of our people to reclaim and insist upon the preservation of our most basic founding principles, there is no limit to our degradation - at any level and in every manner - simply under the artfully-executed banner of *selective-indifference.* Yes, in the last chapter of this volume, I do provide a penetrating synopsis of precisely what *Valor in Prosperity* intends to convey. However, I'm suggesting that you, intuitively, already possess both the understanding and its meaning.

"I HOLD THE IMAGE, I DARE NOT BREATH NOR STIR THE STILLNESS OF PERFECT THOUGHT. WITH NO FRAGRANT LUSTER NOR CURVE OF BRUSH BUT WITH ONLY AN INSTANTS FLASH DID IT APPEAR TO FILL THE VOID WITH ITS CARESS. STRONGLY IT SUMMONS ME TO BECOME MY HEARTS DESIRE SPOKEN IN THE PULSE AND RHYTHMIC LANGUAGE OF DIVINE LIGHT. DO NOT AWAKEN ME, I HOLD THE IMAGE, I DARE NOT BREATHE NOR STIR THE STILLNESS OF PERFECT THOUGHT, THE PERFECT DREAM."

Our world has breached the true meaning of what is *freedom* and what constitutes its expresser, *liberty.* In their place we have become appeasers of spontaneous impulse and situationally-adaptable mores. I find it very difficult to reconcile both *freedom* and *liberty* as companions of impulse for one, if only, significant reason: Although you may be *free* to express, there are prohibitions that might otherwise restrict one's *liberty* to do so.

Society's expressions of excess, in all its forms, are not expressions of *freedom* or *liberty* and are more often only representative of their suppression and emblematic of a societal shift away from their preservation. Consider the explosion of extreme sports, pornography, violent crimes, child abuse, body modification, political schemes, political graft and corruption, tech-addiction, etc. — all of which are expression of an internal void seeking external gratification, or more simply put: *An external expression of an internal condition.*

As in the era when the most conspicuous failings of the Roman Empire appeared we observe very similar indulgences such as the events featured in the coliseum which became increasingly extreme and, yes, more vulgar. Accommodating these extremes was the domain of the government as its own structure was deteriorating and this form of *media* became an effective means for anesthetizing the people. Thus, indulgence of impulse becomes the means by which *freedom* and *liberty* collapse into anarchy and where there is no adherence to and imposition of a constructive adherence to *form,* there is no practical, relevant and stabilizing *function.*

As the human mind is not capable of holding two thoughts, conditions or emotions simultaneously, neither can the human condition assume two completely different constructs simultaneously. In other words, it is not possible to have *duty* and *impulse* occurring at the same time. Even more to the point; when our conscience is captured by the exercise indulging the impulse of external physical gratifications we are not free to harvest the product of inspired thought which occurs only through the discipline of communing with a *higher presence of mind*! After all, as Aristotle professed,

> *"We are what we repeatedly do; excellence*
> *then is not an act, but a habit."*

Not so long ago I was driving back from the airport and once north of the San Francisco Bay I decided to take a side road hoping to navigate around the inevitable afternoon gridlock. I was driving east in the opposite direction when I noticed a man standing on the westbound side of the road frantically waiving as people drove by. I continued on for a moment or two and just as I was beginning to ascend a slight rise in the road I checked my mirror one last time and there he was; no one had stopped. I was rushed and had deadlines and commitments to meet so I continued on, but only for a moment — I've been in his spot before.

I turned the car around and rushed back over the hill I had, only moments before, traversed. As I had only passed a mile or so and I didn't have that far to travel, yet ahead of me were two semi-trucks blocking my view and I was unable to see if he remained. It wasn't long before I came upon the stalled vehicle; the car was there but the man had gone.

After few moments another and then another and yet another automobile pulled up behind mine and each driver emerged from their vehicles and approached. One of the drivers, a nicely dressed woman, asked, "What happened to the man who was standing here?" The others, with equal curiosity, looked at me expecting a response and I simply said, "I dunno, I only just arrived!"

Interestingly enough, as it turns out, each of us had deadlines and places to be yet each turned around recalling that we'd been in this mans place once or twice in the past. Stranger still, no one seemed to express any sense of urgency to leave.

A few moments passed and then a Highway Patrol Officer pulled off behind the row of cars. He walked up to the four of us standing on the side of the road and asked the obvious question, "Do any of you want to tell me what's going on here?" One of the other drivers delivered the story and the officer looked at this rather curious group of people and said, "You're kidding, right?" He returned to his patrol car, flashing lights on, and backed up 20 or so feet and there he remained.

It wasn't long until a pick-up pulled off the road and came to a stop in front of the stalled vehicle. Out jumped the driver who walked to the back of his truck, pulled out a gas can, smiled at the four of us and without a break in his step, walked toward the rear of the stricken car and began to fill the fuel tank. A moment later the man who I'd seen standing on the side of the road appeared from the passenger side of the pickup and stood there emotionless as each of us asked if he was okay or if he needed anything. He just shook his head and said, "Nope, I'm set, but you know what, this is the strangest thing, not ten miles back I'd stopped to help a guy who had run out of fuel and look at me now, I'm standing in his same shoes." He paused for a moment, smiling as he shook his head, then looked at me and said, "You know what's even more bizarre?" Pointing to the driver of the pickup, "He's the guy I stopped to help! Each of you reminded me of something today: the hand the reaches out, reaches farthest! Today it caught…" as he counted the heads around him including his own and the officer, "… seven people headed in all sorts of directions yet willing to stop long enough to make a difference. My father always said, when it matters, you stop and take care of what needs taking care of, that's when it counts most."

It was a good day to be reminded of an old lesson, once again.

By the way, I'm counting on each of your heads too!

And so, once again, on behalf of myself, its author, and

The Imperfect Messenger Foundation

I present to you:

Blind Vision
Volume III
Valor in Prosperity

Enjoy!

Curtis C. Greco

Valor in Prosperity

A DECLARATION

"I've no need for vision to see what I know to be true."

HISTORY CHRONICLES man's long struggle for the ideal of self-determination and expression. The stern opponent to this ambition is oppression which, in its many forms, is our mortal enemy and whose malignant nature has been examined by a great many from Aristotle's dialogues, the Magna Carta, John Locke to Thomas Payne's "Rights of Man" to name but a few.[1] Each of these chronicle and give countenance to the evolutionary progression of man's desire to define, once and for all, his standing among men. However, there is one facet to this prism of thought that I suspect for many may yet be more important than these; our standing with the only Superior from whom all things are derived. That superior *Being,* as referenced in all of the writings I've previously mentioned, or as in the case of the Magna Carte, is none other than God[2] himself.

The implication of these inquiries is not to consider but to affirm that man is not chattel nor are his rights derived by or from any man, monarch, despot or form of government. The affirmation is refined further by declaring that as a matter of fact said *rights* are conveyed only by *nature* itself. Thomas Jefferson expressed this declaration quite specifically and conspicuously and it remains, for all time, a fundamen-

---

1   These references are not intended to be conclusive but merely to illustrate a progression of intention and thought.

2   One might also substitute the reference "Creator," as used by Thomas Jefferson, should the G word trouble you.

tal core of the American ethos. His understanding appears in *The Declaration of Independence* in this way: "… are endowed by their Creator with certain unalienable Rights, that among these are life, liberty and the pursuit of happiness."[3] It is interesting to note that Mr. Jefferson's original draft included the word "property" in lieu of "happiness," which is as it appears in John Locke's[4] Second Treatise.

An extension of this ideal is that man's freedoms are *ex Deo*, i.e., from God, and all that is a product or extension of those freedoms (as long as they do not violate *natural law*) are sovereign to and not severable from the individual. These are not inchoate concepts; in fact, these are the very principles to which the Constitution of these United States is bound to protect and to insure their preservation from *all enemies foreign or domestic.*

I find this all quite exhilarating! A form of government, for the very first time in human history, crafted specifically on a foundation such as this! Not only could the rights of a person not be infringed upon, the product of their labor could not be expropriated. A person was, for the first time, not only presumed by law to be sovereign, the law was charged to insure (safeguard) their *sovereign rights.*

In essence, this Declaration affirmed that you were and are, in effect, a sovereign entity in control and command of not only your corporeal form but also your thought, your speech, your privacy, your property, your faith, your means of safety, your industry and the fruits of your labor to name but a few. The Constitution then becomes, in effect "by

---

3   The entire text of the Declaration of Independence is included in Appendix I.

4   John Locke is a 17th century philosopher. He authored many commentaries on various social, political and economic issues that became the reference for many, and most visible in Thomas Jefferson's most lasting effort, The Declaration of Independence.

the consent of the governed," the vehicle that administrates the collective rights but only within or to the extent of its "enumerated powers" and nothing more. It is, by construct, its guardian. The *Preamble* sets the tone of its design and its purpose:

> *"We the People of the United States, in Order to form*
> *a more perfect Union, establish Justice, ensure domestic*
> *Tranquility, provide for the common defense, promote*
> *the general Welfare, and secure the Blessings of Liberty*
> *to ourselves and our Posterity, do ordain and establish*
> *this Constitution for the United States of America."*

It is so very important to grasp this critical point! You (we) grant the existence of the government; WE, "The People...ordain and establish this Constitution for the United States of America." As Mr. Jefferson said,

> *"The sheep are happier of themselves than*
> *under the care of the wolves."*

Insuring the economic prosperity of any country requires the principle understanding and existence of several critical components. Accepting in advance that I may bring upon myself the ire of many for stating so, I tender the belief that none is more critical than[5] *property rights* and the *rule of law*, specifically, contract law (the later being particularly relevant when applied to the *social contract* that exists between the *consenting governed* and their government.) This is so much a part of our

---

5   Consider that in my use of the phrase, "none is more critical," I specifically intend the reference applied as a core attribute in/to the discussion on Valor In Prosperity. To be sure, there are other necessary components integral to a functional structure such as a medium of exchange, monetary policy, banking system, legislative functions etc, many of which are discussed herein as well as throughout Volumes I and II of the series.

economic culture that for Americans it is a foregone conclusion, to the point that we no longer question the validity and binding nature of a transaction.

THE CULTURE OF PROSPERITY:

When one, as an example, picks up the phone or emails an online order, the assumption that the party on the other end will not perform is rarely, if ever, considered. The process plays out thousands upon thousands of times a day; the free exchange of your property or labor for that of another's property or labor - a topic we discussed at great length in Volume II: *Value Given, Value Received.*

In our current age of electronic transactions, the clarity, the certainty of this profound act has seemingly become a systemic and unquestioned necessity and should a wayward merchant appear, the court/law, as an impartial advocate, is there to adjudicate a remedy. The enduring strength of an economic system is proportional to these *absolutes* and the unbiased manner in which they are perfected.

> "THERE WILL NEVER BE A FREE MARKET RESPONSE TO
> A GOVERNMENT CONTROLLED ENVIRONMENT."

To digress for the moment, with your indulgence, I believe it is important to interject a considered observation. It was never the intent of the Constitution to enable the federal government to do anything but provide, i.e. to be the guardian of, the framework where the enterprise can peaceably and equitably take place. Yes, I'll even go so far as to *regulate*[6] the process but never to become an impediment to the practice consistent with its intended design, that is, as a framework for advocacy. *To legislate only and to the extent provided for by the Constitution and/or as conveyed by The People - only and always with absolute deference to the rights of the same.*

It is not my intention to confer upon myself the status of legal scholar—I readily admit I am not—however, I confess to a measured degree of understanding on this topic as I have, for many years, studied the historical fabric of the Constitution, its authors and their writings. It is my opinion that the government has an unholy alliance with the judicial system the nature of which indicates significant strides away from founding principles rather than a determined march toward their preservation. I firmly believe this to be an amorphous coalition that has long been the demonstrated adversary[7] of our *founding ideals*. An example of this is demonstrated by the Supreme Court decision in the case Kelo v. City of New London (2005), which, arguably, vacated the historically sacred protections proffered by the *Fifth Amendment* by further affirming the intrusive right of government *taking* of private property.

When viewing the perspective of the Constitution and its *enumerated powers* one might find the document rather ambiguous and vague and I readily admit it may appear this way. However, such is not the case; it is, in point of fact, absolutely specific. It is not to be understood in the

---

6   Regulate: At the time of the Constitutions drafting, the word "regulate" meant "to make regular" as in the tenor of a more contemporary term, as in the case of the word: "normalize". It did not mean to control, to restrict or to command, which has become the bias of choice when interpreting the Constitutional provisions of Article I, Section 8, Clause 3 known as the *Commerce Clause*.

7   Judge Andrew Napolitano's "The Constitution in Exile: How the Federal Government Has Seized Power by Rewriting the Supreme Law of the Land," as well as his other writings, are must reads! This fine man elucidates many examples of these various legislative and judicial aberrations.

context of *inclusion*, that is, all possible permutations and eventualities. It is a document of explicit *exclusions*; that is to say that the government is *excluded* from engaging in any possibility *not specifically enumerated therein*. It, the government, is specifically restricted! Could it be that the Justices are unaware of the *Federalist Papers*[8] and *The Declaration of Independence?* I find them a fabulous resource for understanding the Constitution and the World Court, supremely irrelevant!

This is just one of the many ways that the government demonstrates its increasingly casual regard not only for its role but its limited function (intended) as well. Whenever a government asserts a claim, whether through interpretation or by fiat, inevitably the net effect is an ever-progressive dilution of its fundamental mandate and an expansion of the arbitrary. The companion to this then becomes a *rule of law* that becomes selectively applied with alarming uniformity and thus, no longer equal justice for all, but only equal justice for the influential and an opaque forum for those with no influence to peddle. Of this, the resource of history reveals the ultimate consequence; a distempered and slave-class people!

"IT IS MORE OFTEN THE CASE THAT THE SYSTEM, AS IT IS, LOOKS
NOT TO ITS STRUCTURE IN ORDER TO PRESERVE AND PERFECT
THE IDEAL BUT TO FIND OR CRAFT MEANS OF DEFEATING IT!"

Are we now to presume that the rule of law is above the absolute of freedom? If this then is the case, are we now then the *subject* of the law and its arbiter? There exists a contrived arrogance in this licentious coterie that has redefined the task of *the law* from a medium

---

8   Federalist Papers: 85 articles authored by James Madison, Alexander Hamilton and John Jay provide a fabulous reference source for understanding and interpreting the U.S. Constitution.

that arbitrates and/or administrates a dispute to the presumption of august patriarch. One should never again be required to surrender to the ascension of the law above that of a stone mason!

> "I'M CONFIDENT IN MY AND POSSIBLY YOUR GOD GIVEN
> DISTINCTIONS OF REASON, AS WELL AS THE MASON'S SKILL AT
> BINDING STONE, BUT THE LAW IS INCAPABLE OF DOING EITHER!"

When I hear the much-used phrase "we are a nation of laws," my first inclination, once I've reclaimed my breath, is to say: *Oh dear God what a tragic legacy.* I'm not entirely sure if this phrase is intended as an excuse, a form of license or simply as a threat! Whatever it is, I'm of the opinion that I'd rather our pronouncement be, instead, that we are *a nation of self-reliant and free people.* Anything that becomes a means to its own end is always wrought with excess and most often at the expense of someone else.

Once again I draw on the clarity of Thomas Jefferson's wisdom:

> *"Our government is now taking so steady a course as*
> *to show by what road it will pass to destruction; to*
> *wit: by consolidation first and then corruption, its*
> *necessary consequence. The engine of consolidation*
> *will be the Federal judiciary; the two other branches*
> *the corrupting and corrupted instruments."*

THE ADVOCATE:

In Volume I of the series, *We Hold These Truths,* there are several occasions where I highlight areas of judicial dysfunction and I suppose they are, topically, adequate. However, considering the previous two paragraphs, one's ability to grasp the message of the current section requires a measured degree of precision. When considering the continuity of *property rights* and the *rule of law,* as neither can be the advocate of prosperity without the acknowledged companionship of the other, clarity on this specific issue is an absolute necessity. It is the silent presumption of what gives life and duration to the topics discussed in Volume II: *Value Given, Value Received* and is the bedrock of *Simple Economics.* I'm counting on your indulgence for a moment or two longer while I address a few more.

The principle of *property rights* and the terrain it covers is comprehensive in nature. In other words, it is not simply the right to own and possess land, which of course it does, but it also encompasses everything that you own or acquire by lawful means as well as, by extension, the faculties of form, function and resources concomitant with the same. It also includes anything, tangible or intangible, that you produce as well as the means or ability you employ to produce it none of which can be subjugated. It becomes, in practice, the very *organic* essence of the *native economy.*

The nature of a true *free market* relies entirely on your ability, your liberty, to sell your *property*, give it away or for that matter, destroy it. The gravity of this fundamental right, particularly in the context of early American history, is to be reminded that under British rule a person was the *subject* (chattel) of the Crown and subservient to its authority. As is the case with all forms of tyranny, it was/is the monarch who granted all rights and privileges and who, at his discretion, could modify, expand or revoke the very same.

A person, in the free and unfettered expression of his/her rights, is then able to set about this enterprise engaging in the free exchange *of* goods and service *for* other goods and services in whatever measure his individual, and that of another's, economy will allow. All of this occurs with the absolute certainty that they, The People, have an ally in the process as an extension of their *will* and as their advocate. The government, then, is to guard this right from or against unlawful practices that may violate this underlying right and arbitrates an ultimate resolution when it occurs.

As history has shown, the marriage of these two fundamental principles ignited a kinetic force from which evolved a very powerful economic engine. Well within one generation of the Founding Fathers, the industry of a *free people,* able to express and develop the unlimited potential of their genius and retain the product and reward of their toil, was proving itself to be quite practical and effective and as we know, it continues to be a model for prosperity around the world.

> "INSPIRATION ONLY BECOMES INSPIRATIONAL WHEN
> PAIRED WITH THE RHYTHM OF INSPIRED ACTION AND
> SO, WHEN MAN'S INSPIRED VISION BECOMES FULLY
> EXPRESSED, IT ALSO BECOMES HIS GREATEST GIFT!"

It must also be understood that the extent to which this model generates prosperity, and the measure of the heights it is permitted to achieve, is largely a measure of how well the model is left alone to achieve it. This ideal has proven to be a marvelous problem solver in the cause of improving man's quality of life - the benefits of which are numerous and clearly visible.

WHY VALOR?:

Prosperity, in its broadest terms and applications, is full of hope and a blank canvas upon which each and every person lays evidence of his ability to uniquely illustrate or express his own sense of satisfaction. For one it may be to become a nurse, another a farmer, a teacher, a scientist and the list goes on and on. To be able to be the *cause* of your own success, uninterrupted and without regard to and without fear of the tyrannical rule of another, is a powerful and motivating force and *most sacred.*

One's prosperity is, in point of fact, correlative to one's absolute sense of freedom and is, most certainly, a measure of it. Freedom however, is not freedom from the integrity that is so vital to our nation's pulse; it is the sworn allegiance to the ideal as being integral to both its lasting form and perfection. In other words, freedom, as described in the underpinnings of our foundation, exists only to the extent one is ever vigilant by insisting upon the ideal as an absolute, *unalienable.* Freedom, when best expressed, becomes that which in the course of your own pursuits impedes not that of another's efforts when engaged in the very same act of expression. Again, as is always the case, the presumption is that your pursuits are *lawful.* By the way, this applies to the government as well.

"WHEN GOVERNMENT NO LONGER DEMONSTRATES AN ALLEGIANCE TO THE IDEALS OF THE PEOPLE FROM WHICH ITS VERY EXISTENCE IS DERIVED, IT ALSO NO LONGER FEARS NOT HAVING DONE SO!"

Yes, there is *Valor In Prosperity*. The republican form of government *is* democracy at its finest. It has been the course on which a people have propelled themselves from the subsistence state of existence to one that has refined the means by which they might be released from so basic a plight. This form has been both a fierce and liberating force as well as a most effective compass. It has spawned the distinctions of capitalism[9] that continues as a beacon and one which people from all over the world are drawn. Why? Simply put, it is an intuitive, organic, native and elementary condition of the *human being*.

Unfortunately so universal an ideal, left to the devises of the lecherous, becomes the means by which it is squandered. It is from the sentiments of the preceding statement that I use the word *valor*. For me, the word speaks of strength of mind, strength of spirit, the nature of which enables a person to encounter a challenge or danger with firmness and resolve. It is appropriate that such a word should accompany the prize of prosperity in all its forms, tangible and intangible!

"THE FAILURE OF GOVERNMENT IS ALWAYS ROOTED IN A
BELIEF THAT ITS POWER IS SOMEHOW THE RESULT OF ITS
PRESENCE AND NOT FROM THE STRENGTH OF ITS PEOPLE'S
LOVE FOR AND PRACTICE OF ENDURING PRINCIPLES!"

---

9   My *distinctions* of capitalism are presented in Volume II of the series: *Value Given, Value Received* and are integral to fully understanding the breadth of the context to which I intend. These *distinctions* are of great value and I encourage their study and discussion.

REVISE AND REDEFINE:

From the birth of this country and even unto this very day, tyranni-cal forces wage a revisionist view of the rights of man. Their mind set evokes the aura of an entitled arcana claiming itself as sole repository of the fuel necessary to perpetuate, successfully, the ideal of self-gover-nance. This then is or becomes the expression on the face of *oppressive government,* one that expresses with an air of contempt *that freedom is largely wasted on the masses.* Whether this is true or not is largely irrelevant in the absence of demonstrated conviction. Nonetheless, to conscript mans rights, regardless of what form, be it your income, your freedom to choose or whatever other extension of these rights one may manifest, is wholly immoral and unjust. The ignoble nature of the beast assumes your apathy as the very means it employs to insure the illusion that government intrusion is necessary to assure your very survival! The beast expresses this illusion by a rather unique and spurious term: *social justice* - the ultimate expression of *selective-indifference.*

The nihilist will say, "Let us take your cow so that we might give you milk!" On his next visit, he then takes your bull as you no longer have a cow. Eventually you learn of the new entitlement, "FEHP" (the Federal Eco-Balanced Hydration Program) and you are gratefully comforted to discover that the messianic government has come to your aid providing you water from the well it confiscated from your neighbor! Not to worry though, you've been assured by the apocryphal notion of *social justice* that this is all being done *for the good of The People!*

Well, a thinking person might ponder: Who exactly are *The People* and who was it that anointed the arbiter and reposed supreme right(s) to determine the same and by doing so, target *The People* for conquest? The Biblical message that "Man cannot serve two masters" is also true for the tyrant government. It also is evidentiary of the causal force relegating The People to servant status. Know of course that this abrogation occurs in very subtle and inconspicuous ways that are artfully crafted in a most deliberate manner and of course, always for the most compassionate of purposes. The following day you awaken to a Brave New World, [10] absent a bit more reason and a bit less property (rights)!

> "IN THE ABSENCE OF CONVICTION THERE IS
> AMBIVALENCE AT WHICH POINT, POSSIBLY, EVEN
> AMBIVALENCE BECOMES AMBIVALENT."

Consider, of course, that one of the great wonders of the republican form of government is that it demonstrates how people of different, entirely different, ideals can work together for a common end. It may well be, within the context of the preceding statement, that the means may lie by which the concept of freedom and the practice thereof might best be understood. It may also be that it is for this very reason people of different ideals must be ever mindful of the need for freedom to persist.

In the robust interchange of ideas that surround the opposing views of a strong central government[11] exists the antithetical view of a strictly limited central government[12] which resolves to the ideal that the majority of government influences be relegated to the individual states and/or to the people themselves. Ultimately in the construct that

---

10   This is a deliberate reference to Aldous Huxley's book by the same title — a wonderful illustration, in words, of the absurd in action.

11   Historically, those favoring a strong central government were referred to as Federalists.

12   Those preferring the strictly limited central government form were known as the Democratic-Republican party which later split, on differences, to the form we have today.

became the Constitution, the latter, evidenced by the Bill of Rights and the 10th Amendment, was clearly the direction of choice.

Clearly anyone with a perspective other than my own will likely resign himself to my possessing a clear bias which, simultaneously, is yet an indication of their own. Nonetheless, my perspective resides fundamentally in the absolute that **no** man has the right to claim or otherwise partition the providential rights of man beyond that which he may temporarily grant or, by the way, revoke. It then follows that the government should operate only to the extent of those (rights) tendered and always tethered by an ever-present tenor of restraint.

INSTITUTIONALIZING INDISCRETION:

Stripping away the trappings of the academician's theoretical arguments, who among us would be willing to surrender his or her right of self-determination or, for that matter, one's unalienable rights to life, liberty and the pursuit of happiness? Now then permit me to ask the question another way. Who among us would be willing to surrender *another's* right of self-determination and all that accompany the same? Would that a politician proposing legislation ask these questions in light of the Constitution and all of its supporting documents.

"WE SEEM, IT WOULD APPEAR, TO HAVE INSTITUTIONALIZED
A NEED TO FAIL. RARE, IF EVER, DOES ONE OBSERVE
THE POLITICAL PROCESS RESTRAINED OR YET HEARD IT
SPOKEN; THIS IS NOT THE ROLE OF GOVERNMENT!"

It is not sufficient to simply say *no* to these questions, it is *more important* to understand the *why* you *must say no*. It is not only that you would never surrender your God given rights, it is that no one, *to a man*, should ever presume to be able to author even the slightest supposition that it was even possible to consider so treacherous an ambition as to conscript another's. I might even go so far as to say that it is to the substance, the core implication of this one paragraph, that the entire *Blind Vision Series* questions.

The great tendency of man is to craft his ambitions and leave his intentions for an uncertain outcome. To wit, the ultimate risk of government, be it federalist or republican, is that the very *outcome* (of legislation) is always in the company of unintended gravity[13]. It is with equal concern that dubious influences can, with equal intention, propagate *intended* gravity. There are several fine examples of the *unintended gravity* illustrated in the opening chapter of Volume II: *Value Given, Value Received* specifically those described under the sub-heading *Government Funding Mechanisms*; there is great value and merit in reviewing each of the items presented. Nonetheless, it remains my opinion that, in its most severe and pervasive form, the most lasting example -and there are several others which (arguably) could be its equal - is the Federal Reserve Act of 1913. President Woodrow Wilson would later lament that he had ever signed this legislation; the effects of which live on to this day.

On this point, it is particularly interesting how the influences of contrived authority, when left unchecked and to its own ends, becomes so absolute and remain so unilaterally unopposed. I speak of government in general terms, I speak of the Federal Reserve in the specific.

---

13   In this instance I deliberately use this word, gravity, to suggest, with acknowledged license, the consequential burden of weight.

Consider if you will for a moment that once (as in the case with economic theory) a political demagogue's theory is placed in practice, every action, event or unintended consequence that occurs from that point on attempts to be explained or expressed in that context. Even more severe is that every possibility for the future becomes constrained by the very same theory.

This is an acutely interesting observation when one considers the present state of the political, social and economic environs of our nation. Every extreme of failure is not associated with the proven inadequacies of its underlying policy; no, the failures are associated with being insufficiently global in their reach and whose repair simply requires just a bit more of the same. A superb example of this systemic and theoretical demagoguery in practice appears in short order and precisely illustrates the point of the following observation:

> "WE HAVE NOT ONLY INSTITUTIONALIZED A NEED TO FAIL, WE HAVE INSTITUTIONALIZED THE METHODS BY WHICH IT HAS BECOME A PERPETUAL OCCURRENCE!"

Government should never be called upon to interpret what constitutes the limits or boundaries of man or his lawful pursuit and expression of his liberties. To do so cements the government position as, simultaneously, both the arbiter and benefactor of the same. I see no action, regardless of how vile, a man might effect which cannot be adjudicated from the boundaries so simply defined in the principles that are contained within the construct that is *natural law*. Otherwise, to descend into the arbitrary and nebulous notions of *selective-indifference*, we unleash the perpetual fabrication of government bureaucracies which, as we have seen, serves only to constrict freedom and redefine the parameters of liberty.

> "THERE IS NO NEED TO LOOK TO FUTURE FAILURES TO CORRECT OUR COURSE; WE'VE ONLY TO LOOK AT THE AGGREGATION OF REASON AND PAST SUCCESSES! THE NATURAL LAW THAT GOVERN EACH OF THESE ARE WHAT DEFINE THE BOUNDARIES THAT ASSURE BOTH SUCCESS AND FAILURE!"

Consider but one (of the many) statement from President Barack Hussein Obama's inaugural address,[14] which provides a particularly keen insight into his own *Pelegian-like*[15] pathology. "The question we ask today is not whether our government is too big or too small, but whether it works - whether it helps families find jobs at a decent wage, care they can afford, a retirement that is dignified. Where the answer is yes, we intend to move forward. Where the answer is no, programs will end. And those of us who manage the public's dollars will be held to account - to spend wisely, reform bad habits, and do our business in the light of day - because only then can we restore the vital trust between a people and their government."

To my observation, with the qualification that this may be uniquely my own, I believe Mr. Obama's overture clearly illustrates my point; in other words, the distinction between *intended* and *unintended outcome* or as I referred to it in a previous paragraph, as *unintended gravity*.

---

14   January 21, 2009. To be fair to the president I include the entire segment so that the impression of *out of context* can be avoided. I must say, I admire Mr. Obama's skill-set, however I wholly disagree with his politics/agenda all of which are in opposition, in both form and function, to the principles of freedom.

15   Pelagious was a late 3rd Century (AD) Ascetic Monk domiciled in Britain. His teaching revolved around the denial of church doctrine of *original sin*. Denying such, he held that people were free to do either right or wrong with no consequence or burden to the outcome of either.

What one should, I trust, elicit from this cue is how the intention of *good government* becomes discretely synonymous with the arcane proclamation of to *do government* by any means and for any purpose.

The consequence of this maze of thought becomes the convergence of deliberately *intended outcome* becoming, for you, *unexpected consequence.* If we were to dissect the entire inaugural address, one will discover a superb example of theoretical political demagoguery expressed in a manner and form like none other before[16] and hopefully, never again. *Therefore, if we are to have any hope of saving ourselves from our near habitual errors in judgment, we must then resolve to the postulate that to be good government one must find an ally in the best possible form; less government.*

Government should not be seen as nor permitted to be the instrument whereby we perceive it as the origin of resource and justice; this must first and always reside in the ambition of the individual to regard these principles as his own and as both an *inseparable mandate* and *unalienable right.* Doing so clarifies the thought that the individual is the impetus of progress and the ultimate resource of cause. In other words:

> "I AM FREE TO SUCCEED AND ENJOY THE REWARDS OF MY SUCCESS AND AM EQUALLY FREE TO FAIL AND ENDURE THE RESULTS OF FAILURE AGAIN AND AGAIN UNTIL I SUCCEED!"

The desire to blend the meddling tendencies of government into so core a sentiment is to then also accept that not only does government

---

16   To provide a fair accounting of historically relevant figures, Dr. Paul J. Goebbels, who was the German Reich Minister of Propaganda from 1933 to 1945, is worth noting. His oratory skills were equaled only by his precise and tactical execution of the audacious proclamation or "Big Lie" method of social indoctrination which simply suggests that the more audacious the lie, the more believable it becomes to the masses.

become the source of one's forward progress, and thereby vested in its results, it also becomes compliant in mitigating the adverse. Further, to perpetuate this viral extension of thought serves only to institutionalize the *cradle to grave* metaphor and the regime that breeds from its distortions. Conspicuous, by example, of this seemingly ever-evolving life-form and its interventionist dogma is the inveterate growth of insidious government. What follows are ten examples, along with added commentary, illustrating my earlier reference wherein I identified how our government has *institutionalized the need to fail!*

1. **FDR's New Deal (circa 1933-38):**

    A series of initiatives promulgated by the Roosevelt administration whose stated intention was to stage a Depression-era recovery; a fine example of socialism-style central planning where the institutionalization and disfiguring effects of progressive practices established precedence for all that followed. However, roulette style planning *by consensus from on high* was ineffective, wasteful and has largely been viewed as a failure. The many subsequent social engineering programs that entered the chambers of public discourse found their way through portals created by FDR's many critical distortions of the Constitution and whose impact continues to scar our social, political and economic landscape.

2. **National Labor Relations Act (circa 1935):**

    Codifies the structure of the collective bargaining process. In 1962 President Kennedy extended the domain of this concept to public employees. Again, in theory, a well-intentioned law, in practice quite specious. In effect, the NLA instigated several stern and destructive practices among these being: (A) Vacated the rights of a person to engage in the sale or exchange of his own property, i.e., his labor. (B) Institutionalized the fracturing of the economic process by mandating the abdication of the individual right to a non-vested enterprise, i.e., the union. (C) Created an undue and excessive burden upon enterprise to indemnify and assure an economic model/cycle that was/is beyond the control of business, or in the case of public employee unions, the government. (D) Regimented the policy of *entitlement* in to the labor pool and social ethos.

As has often been the case, the administrating body of the union becomes a beast unto itself with greater regard for its own *end* than that of the group it is intended to serve. The government could have simply legislated an industry-specific "tiered minimum wage and work week statutes" and left enforcement of work environment mandates to the states and the existing judicial process.

3. **Supreme Court / "Separation of Church and State" (circa 1962):**
    The Constitution deals with the issue from the perspective of the government in the context of freedom *of* religion, i.e., the First Amendment: "Congress shall make no law respecting an establishment of religion, or prohibiting the free exercise thereof." Taken within the context of history and the totality of intention evidenced by the abundance of written text on the subject by and between the founding fathers and their practices while engaged in the function of their duties, it is an escape from all reality to suggest that they meant or intended the interpretation to be freedom *from* religion. I've read volumes of opinions on the subject and am cratered by the selective and disjunctive use of the overwhelming preponderance of evidence that would suggest otherwise.

The framers, as will any sane person, recognized that civil society prospers when restrained by a regard for providential law[17]. To excise the ideal from civil discourse is to leave its benefits to coincidence. To suggest that any individual's actions are not governed by a moral code while in the practice of their lives is to ignore the distinctions identified in the opening sentences of *The Declaration of Independence.* The equivalent thought in the abstract is best illustrated by the use of the *Seventh Commandment: Though shalt not steal;* a moral code that without which, as a basic tenant of social order, there would be none.

Lastly, I believe lost in the various interpretations of the Constitution, as well as the collateral commentaries of those who drafted the same, is this: It was understood that what was being created (government) was an inanimate entity and thus being so had not the means with which to animate unto itself a religion or engage in its distinction or its practice. It then would follow that the government should never determine, by reason or arbitration, the distinction of one religion from that of another. The *Founders* however did know and expect that men of moral standing and with deference to *Providence* would be called upon to express, unto their highest purpose, the practice of sound government. They, particularly Jefferson and Franklin, though not to the exclusion of others, knew that the enduring hope of freedom would rely on this very expectation of moral standing and fiber. Nearly to a man was the common understanding and practice of the precepts of the Judeo-Christian ethos. To suggest that they gave no consider-

---

17   Providential law, as I intend, refers to *natural law*. *Natural law*, in a more commonly identified form, is often associated with Mosaic law. In the matter of all my references to *God*, simply accept that I intend to mean said *Being*, whose existence and form is incapable of being fully understood and quantified by man. However, one should not construe this to mean or imply that *It* does not exist.

ation to the belief that the moral health of the nation could not sustain itself far from so fundamental a code, regardless of what religious sect one might assign them to, is soundly unsupported by the facts.

4. **United Nations: Founded in 1945:**
    Again, in the domain of the altruist, a warm and fuzzy ambition; however an unsupportable notion when contrasting the far-reaching influences of this body upon the people of the United States. If we are to retain the principles defined in our Constitution, then these are universally incompatible with the stated intentions of the United Nations and those who would use it as well as its *sister operative* the International Court of Justice (aka *The Hague*). In no area that I can identify have the people of the United States benefited by participation in this enterprise. Though, to be fair to the argument, there have been countless enterprising individuals who have. My own anecdotal reference for the U.N. is expressed in this way: *A coming together to insure a falling apart!*

5. **LBJ's "Great Society" (circa 1965):**
    A collection of legislative acts, some quite well intended and meaningful; however, taken as a whole, the institutionalizing of mediocrity is, by itself, supreme evidence of government social engineering at its absolute worst. *Unintended gravity* by generational disfiguration.

6. **Community Reinvestment Act (circa 1977):**
    Signed into law by President Jimmy Carter and yet another example in the extreme that typifies the institutional and malignant effects of government by conscription. The CRA was intended to address deteriorating inner cities by forcing Banks and Savings and Loans

to selectively target areas of interest. This legislation was made far worse in its effect by subsequent legislative acts that further metastasized its lethal influences upon the banking system and housing industry. The Act remains a *poster child* for wretched excess and masterfully executed government mismanagement.

7. **Internal Revenue Code (circa 1939 et seq.):**
    I worked in the public accounting profession in the first 12 or so years of my professional life and I confess that I find nothing salvageable in this compendium of codified and seemingly unending examples of conflagration, cross-purposes and near infinite ambiguity. An example of this is the pervasive use of tax credits for the selective endorsement of economic bias. A case in point is the earned-income credit which enables a person who, even if having no effective tax liability, may receive as much as a $5,600 direct tax-credit refund. Government obviously requires revenue to fund its various functions but this is not how it should be done. This approach is the epitome of failure exceeded only by the unwillingness of the elected to address it. (Note: There are wonderfully relevant discussions on this subject in Volume II: *Value Give, Value Received* as well as later on in this volume under the chapter: *A Functional Stimulus.*)

8. **Roe v. Wade (circa 1973):**
    Here is an example where the final promulgation of the Constitution, which I'll simply paraphrase as "those rights not enumerated herein are left to the individual States and to the People," can be juxtaposed to the expansive risk of over-governance.

    First, let me un-categorically confess that I am a *pro-life* advocate simply from the vantage point of the *intended-design* perspective which I express in this way: Who would deny the purpose of the procreative act as being anything other than for the purpose of creating life? The design of the action is also its intention. At the point of convergence of the woman's egg and the male's semen, which up to and until that point are individually benign, the function of their design is perfected. Is it not? If so, and I cannot conceive of a perspective that could interpret otherwise, then how could the product of this convergence be anything other than evidence of life itself? As the Court did not necessarily suggest otherwise it did introduce the notion of what constituted life in the abstract term of "viable", that is I presume, viable as it relates to the ability of the fetus to persist outside the womb of the mother. How preemptive and *selectively-indifferent* can you get? Yet, regardless of this convenient predilection, abortion is what it is and what it *is,* amounts to the *taking of life.*

Still, that is not my problem with Roe v. Wade. My issue with the Court's decision is this: The Court's decision removes from the exclusive domain of the individual what it can and might do with her/his body and by decree, institutionalizes a standard of governance as to not only what constitutes life, but what constitutes its viability. In effect, the Court subrogates *Providential Design* to discretion and by doing so, summarily assigns the government the ability to discern and thus burden an entire nation with a universal decision that willfully endorses an inevitable conflict with every individual's sanctity of life ideal as well as one's standing before their Creator. In other words, enforced sanctioning of an *evil that men do!* Shameful!

An unholy precedence that illustrates, once again, how the Court can be the stooge of bias and one that degrades the moral fabric of a nation. I may not agree with abortion and clearly I don't, but I agree far less with government imposing itself in so divisive a manner. At best, the Court should have said it had no jurisdiction in the matter and referred the matter to the individual states. At worst, exercised judicial restraint by simply affirming the right of choice, specifically restricting government sanction of any kind, leaving discretion to the individual(s), his/her conscience, the advise of their clergy and/or physician.

9. **Various Trade Agreements:**
    WTO, GATT, NAFTA, CAFTA et seq. (circa 1995 and after): These agreements illustrate the unique nature of government when the uniformed and the ill-intentioned become co-conspirators. Believe it or not, I've read every one of these agreements and at the conclusion of reading and studying each I was left with one overwhelming thought: An American of conscience could not possibly have written this and no true American could have voted for them.

    If the concept of racism can be applied to a document as a means with which or by which a people are disadvantaged, then these each illustrate racism and bigotry in the absolute extreme. Not only are they biased, they are a wholesale disembowelment of this nation's economic engine and the subversion of our national sovereignty in so many ways that I scarcely know where to begin or end. Trade works when participants equally benefit and the title of Volume II: *Value Given, Value Received* and its entire discussion is dedicated to the *unalienable right* of the individual to be master of his own economy as it is a direct extension of his corporal form and may never be subjugated. Anything less, or more for that matter, is piracy by one and degradation for the other. Ignorance in action is no excuse for the complicity required in so damaging and arguably, so treasonous an act(s). (Note: In both Volume I and II of the series, I present several discussions on the issue of *globalism* which each of these trade agreements is integral to. Needless to say, I recommend their review.)

10. **Patriot Act (circa October 2001):**
    September 11, 2001 will live for all time in the collective memory of our national conscience. On that morning, I was preparing to leave for the office and as I am accustomed to do, I had the television turned to my favorite news channel instantly becoming transfixed by the live events of that morning. Nothing but vigilance could have prevented the focused efforts of these Muslim fanatics! Proof of our reason for fearing and objecting to *big government* is the proven *fact* that it was this very overfed beached whale's ineffectiveness and misdirected lethargy that ignored the signals and numerous opportunities to detect and prevent the event from occurring. Before rushing to create yet another labyrinth what should have been done (first) was to correct the error, not to add to its inveterate abuses and sclerotic agility.

    Since its enactment, it has perfected the art of impulsive failure and abuse which will continue until such time as the *Act* is repealed. There is no other solution.

    The endeavor we think of as freedom will never be perfected by its surrender. *Ever!* Benjamin Franklin understood the fundamentals that lie behind this observation when he stated,

"The man who trades freedom for security does
not deserve nor will he ever receive either."

I suppose that at this juncture it would be appropriate for me to pose a question: When taken as a body of work, which, if any, of these can be viewed as inseparable from the cause of freedom and prosperity? In their totality, can we honestly claim any of these as a success? Yes, there are components of one, possibly two, of these examples and I cede the point but only to the occasional few yet looking for the few doesn't quite mitigate the overwhelming failure each of these represents. To burn down your home in order to cure an infestation of insects doesn't quite seem to be a particularly intelligent approach or one worthy of acclaim. One could only imagine what senseless legislation would evolve from the artifice of government when presented with the need to resolve a traffic snarl at a four-way intersection. I'll not waste time conjugating the details; however, if one were to simply imagine the obverse of, in its most extreme, the simplicity of installing a *stop sign,* one will likely arrive at the point I intend.

TO WHAT PURPOSE?

At this point one might be inclined to ask: *To what purpose these commentaries?* Simply, my belief is that we as a People need to be reminded of our collective history and of the foundations upon which this nation is based. These are not only historical, they are in point of fact, historically significant! We have a duty in our time to engage in the enduring struggle required to secure each and to once again *pledge our sacred honor* as an oath to future generations, to one another and to our predecessors who, as Abraham Lincoln so passionately stated:

"…shall not have died in vain — that this nation,
under God, shall have a new birth of freedom —
and that government of the people, by the people,
for the people, shall not perish from the earth."

Like me, I imagine that many of you have also walked the many historical battlefields, military cemeteries and national memorials. However there is one in particular, Gettysburg, which draws my attention most. The images of the fallen, as it has for many, strain my emotions completely! The ideals of freedom are worthy of our best efforts even if it should require one to protect this very ideal from the divisive intention of one's own countrymen; by doing so, in truth, we preserve and protect both. So it is that we are indeed called upon to take up the standard that bears the banner of freedom and march toward a certain destiny where all men, for all time, shall be free of tyranny and its many disguises.

From this alignment of thought I believe, in part, that central to the preservation of freedom is the restoration of the ideal of self-reliance. To wit one might ask: What then are the parameters of self-reliance? To begin: It is faith first in your innate compass that all men possess, more or less. This compass becomes the rudimentary component that equips each with the ability to distinguish, with the heart of your yearning, the cognitive precepts that embody the command of what is *right* and the prohibition of and against what is *wrong* and the compelling will to ascend to the former. These are, summarily, the domains of the animate of man and vacant in the inanimate of government. Further, it is important that we move far beyond the simple distinction of *self-reliance* to that of an equally important and companion distinction, this being the idea of *self-sustaining*.

As a forum for expanding upon this point, i.e., *self-sustaining*, I will count on your temporary indulgence by permitting me to slightly modify the conventional teachings of the Ten Commandments. I accomplish this by slightly altering the traditional presentation from "Thou Shalt Not…" to something a bit more explicit. To that end, at least for this purpose, I will restate the syntax to appear as, instead, "Thou *Canst* Not…."

What then follows from this slight modification of the traditional form is the discovery, perhaps, of a meaning lost somewhere along the way by the various translations originating, likely, from the original Aramaic text. Again, from "Thou shalt not…" to "Thou *canst* not…." In so doing we expose the point I hope to make which is this: That regardless of what you may do, you can never make it *so*. That one can never perfect what is not possible to ever *be*.

Abstract, perhaps, if so then I might suggest that we consider the following: In the case of "Thou Shalt Not Steal," in its simplest inter-pretation it simply offers the prohibition that one should not take what is not his. Applying the temporary *modification*, the Commandment then becomes: "Thou Canst Not Steal."

What then is the distinction created by the insertion of the word "Canst" in lieu of the traditional term "Shalt"? Simply this: One might steal something from another and take possession of it, *but* and in spite of your nefarious acquisition, the stolen object will *never be yours. Ever!* It will forever remain stolen and its effects will be lasting and even if one where to return the stolen item, nonetheless and even if one were to do so, it will forever be recorded in time as having been *stolen*. Here then, we have a view of what becomes of lasting consequence.

With this thought refined, now insert the word *freedom,* or the word *liberty!* It resonates in this way: Thou Canst Not Steal Freedom! Thou Canst Not Steal Liberty! Why again? Because no matter what you *think* you may be doing, you canst *never* take and make your own that which is *not yours!* This is both *perfection* and also an acute exhibition of how one must interpret the concept of *inalienability (i.e.,"unalienable rights").*

I'm fascinated by this observation, specifically as a means with which to expand and better understand the discussion relating to self-reliance. Particularly in the scope of the actions one engages in whilst in the processes of being self-reliant!

In order to fully understand that there are always consequences to any and every decision or choice we make, one must also accept that though we might have control over the domain of choice, we most definitely are unable to alter or control the outcome or the ill-effect it may have upon another. More precisely, that implicit in one's choice is the acceptance that your decision is, indeed, inextricably linked to an outcome. Therefore it also follows that one cannot abdicate responsibility for the consequences of one's actions upon another simply on the grounds of ignorance. Though ignorance may seemingly have no identity, it most definitely leaves a footprint. Jesus himself understood and identified, ostensibly, this very imprint when he pleaded, "Forgive them Father for *they know not* what they do!"[18]

This is yet another reason for the stern objection to the aberration that is *big government* whose ill-conceived actions become the effects which become lost to the consequence of eternal ignorance.

---

18   Luke 23:24

"WE THE PEOPLE BECOME FOREVER LABORED BY THE
UNKNOWN GOOD INTRUSIVE GOVERNMENT SILENCES!"

The interconnectivity of man with consequence is so absolute that to permit compulsive legislative authority (by government) and to enforce its burden upon the People is, once again, to void all boundaries of reason.

This is why collectivism[19] does not and will never work. The fundamental principle on which it is found is also its fundamental flaw. The *one shoe fits all* metaphor works nicely in the abstract of idealisms. However, it is also why the notion of *Valor in Prosperity* is an anathema to *collectivist* thought. There is no middle ground in nature. There exist no almost-freedom, there is no partial liberty and there is no partial prosperity.

"THE MOMENT ONE TAKES A PIECE OF ANY THING,
THE IMAGE OF WHAT CONSTITUTES ITS STRUCTURE
NO LONGER RETAINS ITS COMPLETE FORM! ALL THAT
REMAINS IS THE MEMORY OF WHAT ONCE WAS!"

The *collectivist* interprets the idea of man's inter-dependence, the so-called *global view,* erroneously and reserves the right to define what becomes of form and structure, regardless of *providential absolutes.* He interprets the concept of *economic engine* as a means of entitlement and the individual as fuel. He believes that prosperity is his to dispense with regardless of the motive force that gives it life. He considers *taking* not as *theft,* but simply *giving in reverse.* The *collectivist* believes in the

---

19   Collectivist or collectivism: I use these terms as a sort of container. I dump all the "isms" of tyranny into this waste-bin identifier, be it socialism, communism, Marxism , etc. In short, any ideology that is the opposite of republican (and I don't mean the Political Party) ideals.

absolute of eugenics,[20] that some are more valuable than others with the unproductive being the more valuable. The body of evidence is unmistakable. The former British Prime Minister, Margaret Thatcher, had a keen sense of this *ism* which is clearly evident in her comment which follows:

> *"The problem with socialism is that eventually it runs out of other people's money to spend!"*

Oh, to be sure, I've made presentation many times in the public forum and it has had its polarizing affects on the erudite who label my commentaries as nothing more than the pedestrian ramblings of a vagrant however these individuals ignore the elementary fact that their offenses are the very evidence proving the absolute of fundamental truths. Or, as William Shakespeare mused, "Me thinks thou doth protest too much!"

It has been my experience that the reason those who oppose *Freedom* and *Valor in Prosperity* are so defiant and vocal is largely due to the fear of losing their influence and the discretionary resources of and for personal gain to which they have become accustomed. An extension of this anecdotal thought can also be applied to understanding why the *collectivist* expressed contempt for and committed opposition to universal rule or to a moral foundation: They fear the exposure of having their practices filtered by the absolute of so formative a structure. They are, after all, the consummate nihilists![21]

---

20   Eugenics: The science or movement of or relating to selective breeding.

21   Nihilism: A viewpoint that traditional values and beliefs are unfounded and that existence is senseless and useless. A doctrine that denies any objective concept of truth, especially, moral truth (Merriam-Webster). A further derivation of the concept gives life to "60's era notion of "bring it all down" for whatever purpose it may suit even if no purpose exists.

I'm reminded of a recent discussion with a good friend; he is a fabulous cook and so in order to maintain favor and access to his board of fare I will simply assign this good man the name *Lee*. Lee and I were discussing a concern over the growing trend of governments increasingly imposing "point of sale" (POS) ordinances. POS is a concept used in a variety of ways but in its basic form, as in this example, it becomes a means for a government entity to enforce a law by placing the burden of its enforcement upon the participant to a transaction the components of which have, by enacting of said law, now become subject to the underlying ordinance.

To illustrate the point, consider the following example: A municipality has likely squandered its operating budget through various financial indiscretions and no longer has the resources to conduct a service traditionally considered their responsibility. To solve this problem a regulation is adopted that states something to the effect that whenever a home/building is sold, as part of the sale process the seller is required to hire a tradesman to inspect a sewer line. If there is any damage to or issues affecting the integrity of the *line* the seller is responsible for paying for the repairs. Lee is of the opinion that the city should have the right to impose this type of POS ordinance. My response to him was simply this: "Which rules do you mean Lee? The rule that defines your rights on which they infringe or the rules that they use which suborn your rights and impose their own will?" Lee, always quick to respond, was about to make a comment however, his senses quickly restored, he succumbed to the domain of reason. He closed his eyes, accompanied by a slight sigh and the upturned corners of his lips. Clearly, reason prevailed over temporary ignorance and I am very proud of him.

The *collectivist* abhors the soundness of principle as it has an annoying way of conflicting with their ambition(s). His preference is the government mandate of selective-egalitarianism whereby we assure success of the *collective* while ignoring the superior right of the individual. This perspective of course is the convenient perspective of privilege whose ignorance insures, ultimately, the collective's failure! Collectivism only serves the self-anointed protectorate and the entitled elite, which in the end, is the grandest of all illusions. These *illusions* appear in nearly every component of one's life and one will do well to remember this point the next time you *Vote for Change.* (Note: Several illustrations of these grand illusions appear throughout this *Series,* although the examples are not confined to these chapters. The most conspicuous appear in: Volume I, chapters *Conflict and Selective Ideals, Economic Implications* and *Social/Entitlement Implications*. In Volume II, chapters *Simple Economics, Monetary Policy* and *The Practice of Money* will provide ample resources as well.)

Thomas Jefferson had a fundamental belief in man's ability to ascend and meet the demands and duties of self-government. Although he clearly had a qualitative grasp as to the means required for self-government to endure, he and his contemporaries also understood that key to its survival was in structuring a form of government that by its nature was limited in its scope of powers and, due to its inherent cameral form, must also navigate through the imposition of its design. In the end, he as well as his contemporaries understood that the ultimate success of self-governance was left to posterity and their vigilant efforts applied to insisting that it be so.

Benjamin Franklin, in response to an inquiry as to what type of government was the product of the Constitutional Convention, is alleged to have replied "We have given you a Republic, if you can keep it." One of his more provocative statements, and he most certainly had many, is as follows:

> *"In these sentiments, sir, I agree to this Constitution with all its faults; if they are such; because I think a general government necessary for us, and there is no form of government but what may be a blessing to the people if well administered; and I believe, further, that this is likely to be well administered for a course of years, and can only end in despotism, as other forms have done before it, when the people shall become so corrupted as to need despotic government, being incapable of any other."*

If we The People truly do subscribe to the ideals and demands that are integral to the beneficial outcomes that accompany prosperity, then our commitment to their faithful practice is mandatory. There is no middle ground and there is no final and complete achievement of prosperity or freedom, it exists only as the product of our persistence and *at any time we may become orphaned by our lethargy.*

Kindly take a moment and reread the previous paragraph. It is so vitally important that the people of this (or any) nation immerse themselves in the dynamic message it intends to convey. It is vital that we capture its message so that we remain faithfully vigilant to an understanding of yet another fundamental truth: It is not so much that collectivists aren't right in their thinking, it is more so that they are simply so very wrong in their adaptation of what was once rational and reasoned thought. They are fallen spirits who no longer find *valor in prosperity* as they have either surrendered or simply lack the creative and adaptive mind required to feed its kinetic force. Instead, they find a tormented delight in orchestrating, both as architect and as chief provocateur, endless attempts at its suppression.

Their advantage is only derived from our surrendering the presumption that somehow we might sustain prosperity's reward based solely on past success; *or* from a sense that we've stored up a sufficient quantity to last; *or* the peculiar feeling that perhaps we've done our share and now it is for another to assume the burden. Relieved, to be sure, if it were only a matter of assigning someone the simple task of taking out the trash or washing the dishes, then we might feel justified in a less than tenacious regard toward our duty and stewardship.

I am prone to wonder that if the first two occupants of the Garden of Eden had been *collectivists,* what must have been their first command? Perhaps the collectivist would have uttered: "Who then shall we enlist to endure the burden of our eating those wretched apples?"[22]

On this point I am reminded of a famous Barry Goldwater "ism":

> *"I would remind you that extremism in the defense of liberty is no vice."* [23]

THE CONSENT OF SILENCE:

As our literary journey nears a critical transition point, it seems appropriate to pause and review a few key points that I trust one has absorbed

---

22   A not too subtle parody on Adam and Eve, the Garden of Eden, and the prohibition on eating of the forbidden fruit,(here suggested to be an apple) in order to remain in the bliss of the Garden.

23   I've been selective, by purpose, in reproducing the senator's statement. Respecting Mr. Goldwater's clarity of thought, the balance of the quote is as follows: "And let me remind you also that moderation in the pursuit of justice is no virtue." Equally relevant.

along the way. Nearing the conclusion of this current segment of the discussion marks not an end, but simply concludes the prelude to the ultimate purpose of my effort. What has been presented thus far throughout the entire *Series* was required in order to set forth a foundation, a framework from which interested Americans might first orient themselves to the task at hand.

As I listen and review the endless body of material generated by the various media outlets, I am struck by one extraordinary observation: The topics of failure are endless and the fear-based entourage of thought is palpable; however, the content as to viable, thoughtful and practical solutions are completely absent. Absolutely nothing of value is offered. I refer to this approach as *shadow-marketing*, which bares the nebulous definition: "content of *it*, ignoring the critique of *why* and the solution or image of *what*!" The whole purpose of this approach is to *stir the pot* using any means necessary in order to excite the masses and to create *traffic*. It is equally important to know that it is not intended to create outcome at all but *to create cause with absolutely no effect.* Our common goal must then be to complete the process: *To show both the reason of cause and to illustrate how, possibly, we might affect and effect.*

With this cause in mind, it has been my deliberate approach to employ a concept I define as *blunt-force-marketing* which is the complete opposite of the *shadow-marketing* approach. The concept is a tool to assist in the focusing of intention: (a). Precisely define your subject parameters – know precisely what *it* is. (b.) Know *why* a solution is required and/or identify the *why* a solution exists. And, (c.) Define that *what* is to be the solution or image by populating multi-front options. Appropriately armed with these three components, one is now capably prepared to execute.

To that end and with the full understanding that they, by now, should be quite familiar to you, I have reassembled a few components to illustrate the core-message of the entire Series. Each individual participant will need to fully understand the importance of each should an interest in reconstituting our governments, our freedom and liberties be our collective ambition. Kindly review the following:

1. As we discussed in Volume I: *We Hold These Truths*, the concepts of freedom are not the arbitrary notions of man but conveyed only from the benevolent will of a *Devine Presence* or *Being* which our founders reference as the *Creator*. These *unalienable rights* are indistinguishable from the cause of the *Creator* and are inseparable from the commands given unto his created (man) and affirmed by and integral to *The Declaration of Independence* and intimated as follows: "…endowed by their Creator…."

2. In this same volume we identified the political device of *The Policy of Conflict* and how our government's republican form has been suspended through the adaptation and practices of partisanship politics and judicial misprision.

3. From Volume II: *Value Given, Value Received*, the concept we identify as *capitalism* is truly and only the extension of a *free person*, freely expressing his or her *unalienable rights* and doing so with a fundamental adherence to the understanding that though one may be *free to express* his interests, he is not *at liberty to express* a right or freedom beyond the point where doing so adversely affects another.

4. In the same volume we revealed that there is nothing mysterious or abstract about a functional economic system or for that matter,

the environment required for it to foster and propagate its beneficial rewards. We identified the tool of coercive legislation to identify how interests (political and business) who fear the *free-market
of choice* use government to both protect and project financial interests adverse to the public trust.

5. Here, in Volume III, we are introduced to the idea that there is
supreme *valor* in man's application of effort while in the pursuit of
prosperity. *This native force is sacred and inviolable.*

6. Also in this volume, we give consideration to the idea that when
we are in the *pursuit of prosperity,* that it is also the very same kinetic force required, simultaneously, to preserve, protect and defend
freedom and *liberty.*

7. *Valor,* in its most supreme state is sufficient in form and force
such that when fully engaged vanquishes all who would oppose,
manipulate or attempt to conscript a free man and his liberties.
The desire for one is also the very same cause that gives life to the
other. They are, in fact, inseparable. They can neither be given,
nor can they be taken away. They are, as with any flame, of the
kind that must be continuously supplied with the fuel that is one's
personal conviction. If asked to define our single greatest failure
as a People, I would be inclined to suggest that in this area, *conviction,* we have been somewhat anonymous.

"OUR FOUNDING PRINCIPLES ARE NOT BROKEN, IT IS OUR
COMMITMENT TO THEIR PRESERVATION THAT HAS LANGUISHED!"

Sun Tzu, a 6th Century B.C. Chinese general, compiled a magnificent
treatise entitled *The Art of War.* He captured, quite possibly, every con-

ceivable tactical maneuver that one might employ whether applied to a military or non-military campaign. I recall that as I considered the totality of his work, one concept seemed most conspicuously efficient and pervasive throughout his chronicle and it is best described in this way: Advantage your position most efficiently by capitalizing on the weakness of your opponent; in this way, you preserve yourself by allowing your opponent to defeat themselves. Sun Tzu expressed it this way:

> *"Making no mistakes is what establishes the*
> *certainty of victory, for it means conquering*
> *an enemy that is already defeated."*

I have no way of knowing whether Abraham Lincoln was a student of Sun Tzu's writings however what should be clear is that he was well acquainted with and understood the inviolable law of consequence. I believe we will all recognize the striking similarities in his (Lincoln's) observation:

> *"America will never be destroyed from the*
> *outside. If we falter and lose our freedoms, it*
> *will be because we destroyed ourselves."*

Observing government as I do and formulating as concise a statement as possible for the purpose of summarily characterizing its rendition, I am, therefore, resolved to the following:

We have become a nation governed by a beast of unlimited powers where The People are permitted only that which is provided for by law. An extension of this twisted form of governance then evolves into and is expressed by the following: That if there is no law prohibiting an action, then by extension it is reasonable to assume license for nearly any action regardless of what form it may take or what fundamental construct of virtue it may violate. In essence, when freedom becomes subjugated by tyrannical rule, along with it (freedom) go the basic principles that evidence its canopy. *By the consent of silenced, we sanction the evil that men do!*

"No thing is free, no thing comes without a price in some form. Freedom or tyranny, you pay either way, the former by your resolve, the latter, with your Liberty!"

I will bring this section to a close with the following questions, each of which, by the way, I fully expect my readership will consider with the appropriate level of care:

1. Do we understand and have we fully accepted the concept of freedom and its responsibilities?

2. Is there a relationship between the practices of a moral and just people and their understanding of freedom? And lastly,

3. Is the degree of freedom a people enjoy directly related to their understanding of and allegiance to a moral and just purpose?

I will leave it to you, the reader, to formulate your own response and accept whatever responsibility to which you may be inspired! Know this: I have faith in Divine Providence and His noble construct among these being: "Life, Liberty and the Pursuit of Happiness." If you find a kinship in these ideals, I extend my faith in you. If not, I'll leave open the idea that it may only be a matter of time before you do. I also acknowledge that God is very, very patient with us and has a remarkable sense of humor.

The following quote is a personal favorite and as I have done throughout the *Series,* I have placed it in a conspicuous location. I believe it aids nicely in expressing the expanse of our collective purpose.

"An American is not only an individual who may find on these shores a companion in Providential Ideals; however, it is truly and only these providential ideals that define an American! It is a pulse that resonates with the rhythm of truth in People of all nations whose hearts beat with the cadence of but one word! Freedom! It is then not only for this union to champion so noble a cause, but for all to assert and ascend to the ideal of freedom, liberty and justice. By dong so, we banish tyranny, in all its forms, to the regime of failure."

Conspicuous by Their Actions

CONSPICUOUS BY ITS ABSENCE amidst the dire mantra of crafted sound bites, vague and indiscreet commentary, is the fertile interchange and color of inspired and constructive thought. It appears as if the body of our combined experience is saddled, frozen with apprehension, awaiting the final blow.

> "JUST BEYOND THE BOUNDARIES OF CONSCIOUS POLITICAL THOUGHT, THE EVIDENCE IS OVER POWERING. WITH LASER-LIKE INTENSITY WE CAN SEE, WITH THE NAKED EYE OF CONSEQUENCE, THE GOVERNMENT ALOOF TO THE PEOPLE'S REALITY!"

To this point: It has been my primary intention to appeal to your sense of historical significance and to regenerate your esteem for the perfection that is republicanism, our representative form of government. The idea is, as I've emphasized again and again, rooted in the sovereign ether of man's highest ideals whose source may be traced to the very fiber of nature's origins. Yet to be fair, one must also acknowledge that we do have the unique ability to muck it all up though lingering simultaneously with this tendency, man does possess a profoundly robust capacity for recovery and near prophetic acts of pure selflessness.

Before us, in this time of American and world history, is the palette of circumstances that mirrors the consequences of choices made. I believe it is time we speak with one voice, act with symphonic precision and a keen sense of purpose; stand and claim our common destiny with reliance on our "robust capacity for recovery and near prophetic-like acts of purse selflessness!"

The magnificent portrait that is nature appears to us only as a study in contrasts, without which there would be no definition or context. Creation is in a constant state of perpetual cycles, each evolving into another, each with its own polarity the components of which, in one form or another, are required to complete the cycle: positive/negative, hot/cold, male/female, matter/anti-matter, life/death/birth and so on.

In the case of government the concept of contrast, for example - order/chaos, I would proffer though historically a cycle, it is not a life-cycle, but one of self-imposed death or contrasts caused, as we have observed, by *extremes* and *excesses*. In the case of the American form of government, the extremes and excesses were intended by design to be excised by the tensions and filtering imposed by the Constitution. The foundation of the Constitution, which we have discussed throughout the *Series,* is so conspicuously absolute that it is only by imposition of *extremes* and *excesses* that it has become distorted.

Beginning in late 2008, the political interpretation of self-government made yet another attempt at self-aggrandizement. Observing the fracturing of the U.S. economy, a new term began to see the light of day: *stimulus package.* Attempting, as the *concubines of excess* will predictably do, to cover the tracks of failure, the solution was not to correct the mistakes of the past but to simply do more of what has proven to expand the *domain of failure.* This stillborn effort was artfully dubbed the *American Recovery and Investment Act of 2009.*

This *Act* will forever be known as one of the most conspicuous acts of lunacy ever devised by the U.S. government and there is no need for me to attempt to devise a rating scale as there are far too many such examples competing for the dubious honor of *number one.*

All this being said, it is quite reasonable for me to say that this entire *Series* has been developed as it has to present to you from this point on, what I consider to be a series of concepts designed to specifically address the key issues facing this country and more directly, key concepts that as a nation, we will, sooner or later, have to address if we are to reclaim what has been lost. You, the reader, may find it interesting to know that I had originally titled the *Series A Functional Stimulus,* though for various reasons I assigned this title to the next chapter of this volume wherein I presents the most significant of my suggested propositions (*Stimulus Concepts*).

"It appears more often the case that politicians are compelled by doing what is wrong as doing what is right, apparently, will leave them speechless."

Why the title *A Functional Stimulus?* Simple; I intend it as a parody on the *government speak of the day* which has adopted "stimulus" as a rallying cry for coercing various forms of *destructive legislation* and *general bumbling.* Tragically, these forms seed only further dysfunction and error in seemingly endless ways. From financial bailouts, congressional abdication of authority on to virtually every other form of government intervention beyond its prescribed limits. We are witnessing further *institutionalized failures* the likes of which will insure unaccountability and assure irresponsible action.

Why should any State (and its residents) that practices legislative and physical discipline assume the irresponsibility of a State, such as in the case of California,[24] that has perfected the complete antithesis of sound governance? This action runs completely counter to the principles on which the country was founded and upon which its unequalled success developed. This is *collectivism* in action and as we've learned from history, the tyranny of reckless and oppressive government is never limited by conscience; it thrives on the hubris of unbridled excess, self-serving interests and perpetual *selective-reward*.

Yes, as I consider the state of our Nation, what I believe we are witnessing is the dying paradigm of economic and political thought. What we all must consider is whether we are going to surrender what remains of our heritage along with it. Still, the *progressive ideology*[25] is desperately attempting to preserve its influence by selling off the last vestiges of its corporal form though seemingly and completely unaware of the truth; it is arming and fueling the very momentum that will ultimately become its hangman. What the progressive ideologues call *signs of recovery* are the last traces of light on a fast-closing door of its tomb. Rest assured it will not willingly surrender to the abyss, although it must ultimately submit to consequence. This, I trust, is our *shared-faith*.

There is virtually a quarry of unlimited proportions from which to mine resources for this topic; however, that being the case I have had to be deliberate in my efforts to confine the various concepts to a narrower scope while hoping to provide a level of detail sufficient to keep from being obtuse. Also I will, with few exceptions, continue to avoid *calling*

---

24   As of 12/31/09, the State of California public debt amounted to $83.5 billion with a projected 2010 budget deficit of $20.7 billion.

25   Progressive Ideology: Interchange at will the circling concepts of collectivism, socialism, Marxism, etc. Yes, there are some progressive ideals that are consistent with republicanism; I do not intend my comments to imply otherwise. Where the many ideals run off the road in opposition to republicanism, then, of course, if these offend the reader know that you offend me as well. That's one of the many wonders of republicanism; we are free to offend one another yet still be cordial.

out the culprits. After all I am not interested in finger pointing, I hope to arouse your interest, your sense of honor, your sense of duty and ultimately, your participation.

Some may summarily dismiss my *Functional Stimuli* as somewhat pedestrian; these objections, if any, will likely come from either (1) those who prefer the status quo, or (2) the individual who finds his or her academic standing a barrier or an impediment to relevant and practical thought. Either way, the true measure, more or less, of the validity of what will follow is the degree to which these comments take residence with practical application and functional resolve. The outcome, whatever it may be, will reside with the final *Arbiter of Truth*. To be most sincere, I rather like the *odds*.

"Yes, there is always imperfection, this is a constant. However there is the certainty of redemption as even our most profound losses or failures are defiantly survivable."

Before moving to the specifics of our *Functional Stimulus,* I believe they will benefit from a surgical attempt at refining the environment or perhaps better said, providing a measure of context. I trust the following discourse will more fluently illustrate why these *Stimuli* are so valuable and incredibly relevant. To that end, let us consider the…

SYSTEMIC REALITIES:

Faded Memory:

> "ALONG THE PATH, AS THE DISTANCE GROWS FROM
> WHENCE I'VE COME, MY COMPASS FAILING, THE PURPOSE
> AND COURSE OF MY JOURNEY BEGINS TO FADE!"

This verse is intended to illustrate what is, for many, not at all an unusual event in the life of any human; in short, as a nation we have managed to miss a waypoint along our path and we have, in effect, lost our collective way. This series has been deliberately organized in such a way as to attempt, in military parlance, a target-reacquisition of our national heritage and the sense of individual responsibility that is required to preserve it. I believe that the political and economic pandemic that exists today is clearly an evolutionary reality whose origins can be traced directly to the early 1900's and continues, although in a more divisive and dangerous form, to the current day. Consider the evolution as the *merging* of two primary intentions creating what I will simply refer to as an *Alliance*[26]. The first intention is economic vice and the second political influence, the merging of which creates a type of *generational-elite*.

This *Alliance*, in practice, becomes the arbiter of social, economic and political conscience in whatever form necessary all the while persisting just below the surface of whatever the *ism* of the day may be instantly adapting to the ebb and flow of the pendulum's swing. This occurs in a uniquely efficient and parasitic way; the parasite feeds off the host in the matter mentioned previously as *the merging* and when the feeding

---

26   Alliance: As I'm prone to get bored with using the same word to describe the same influence (as you know by now) I tend to use many different *identifiers*. In this case, I use the word *Alliance* simply to identify the totality of converging interests and influences.

has run its course, the process moves to latch on to the next, emerging *ism*. More on what I mean by *ism* in due course.

The product of this evolutionary structure has cultured a predictable cycle where one *ism* ultimately yields and is replaced by yet another. I speak of *Marxism, Leninism, Communism, Socialism, Fascism, Collectivism* and *Progressivism.* Each of these, more or less, evolves out of a perception of social or economic injustice only to become yet another injustice. A view of history indicates how these altruistic and often militant uprisings ignited only to form yet another new *ism*. Ultimately, these congeal to replicate the alleged injustice they intended to replace by substituting a new system whose only (primary) difference is evidenced by the brutality of its grip. The most conspicuous examples are: Czarist Russia, which became the Soviet regime, Weimar Germany became the Nazi regime, the Italian constitutional monarchy became *Fascist,* and British constitutional monarchy, demonstrating the heartiness of its moral courage by standing-down the Nazi threat and without so much as a whimper, transfigured in to its own unique brand of *Socialism.*

In the United States, we have also been steadily marching along the path toward our own unique conversion, *Republicanism* to *Progressivism (Socialism).* It is only because of the precision of the American form of government that the process has been slowed. The Founding Fathers understood the *parasitic risks* quite well and crafted the best, bar none, form of government possible to void the parasite's destructive tendencies. The fact that the republican form, to the extent that it does, still exists at all is but a lone voice affirming these gentlemen's genius.

Unfortunately, the *Alliance* has identified the only weakness of its design and has created an extraordinary method with which to circumvent the structure. What is the weakness? The *contract* between the consenting governed and their government who, on its own, is beholden to the implied trust of said contract. How is the weakness exploited? Quite simply: It ignores the contract and in so doing, it also ignores the will of *The People* and make no mistake, this occurs at all levels of government including the judiciary.

In earlier *volumes* I have presented various indicators elucidating this convergence of intentions: *Coercive Legislation* and *The Policy of Conflict and Selective Ideals* being examples. I encourage all to pay very close attention to the dialogue of the day, whether in print or in the media, when forming your own opinions or resolving to your own sense of conviction; consider using these *Three Truths* as a compass for your thoughts:

I.

"When shaping the rules of operation, the master crafts only prohibitions that conform to his or her intention."

II.

"The torment of any ideologue is the risk that the obstacle of conscience will stall a speedy conquest."

III.

"Influences resolve to only two possible courses: that which stands on the soundness of reason or that which is imposed by derelict thought and resolves so unopposed."

Why do the *isms* ultimately fail? There are many possible reasons of course however, if we resolve to the root cause it is most often due to some form of structural degradation, more specifically, a progressive acquiescence to a fundamental belief that defies (or attempts to) the divinity of the human spirit. The divine human spirit will not suffer a tyrant for long. Why and how has the American republic moved to the point of extinction? I believe the answer, in part, lies in the opening quote of this section.

"WE LOOSE OUR COMPASS AND REPLACE IT WITH INDIFFERENCE; DOING SO, VOIDS OUR NOBLE CONSCIENCE AND LICENSES THE ABUSE OF IMPOSITION."

In Volume II: *Value Given, Value Received*, we identified this malaise-like state as *practical detachment* which is nothing more than the systemic notion that removes from one's state of mind any and all precepts of conscientiousness or rectitude as to duty or personal responsibility and replaces the structure with the notion of entitled license and presumed indifference as to consequence. The notion is most evident in any practice as in the case of, for example, government whereby the legislative process marches on to a presumed conclusion without regard to Constitutional prescription and the will of the People — knowing in advance that it will not be challenged for having done so. One observes a version of the same in the case of a presidential *Executive Orders* that clearly breaches the authority of the president.

In the case of the judiciary, a similar breach occurs frequently where the Court adjudicates a decision not based on Constitutional mandate as an article of precedence, but on one that redefines and ultimately becomes a rule unto itself. In short, who then is to challenge a structure that defines for itself what is to become of that which gave birth to its very existence? Good question! (Note: To enhance the significance of the current topic might I suggest a quick review of the section entitled "Monetary Policy" appearing in Volume II: *Value Given, Value Received.* The correlative value to this [above] unique perspective is quite palpable.)

CORPORATE GOVERNANCE:

In the present era we observe the near-complete transformation of two distinct components of order. Each made the success of the American experiment inevitable by insuring the other. We had a form of government that was confined to its *purpose* and a business model of *capitalism* that began to perfect its form by *practice.*

For the many reasons discussed in earlier volumes, this structure worked fabulously until diversions from further perfection, by way of the "merging" process mentioned in *We Hold These Truths* and refined in *Value Given, Value Received* began to take hold. As the conversion process continued, the intended form and model began to fracture primarily from the emerging dysfunction; the new *ism* which became known as progressivism. This crafted ideal began to use its growing muscle by anesthetizing The People by seeding a growing appetite for ever more *ism*-like rewards and as we know, each new perversion of the truth only yields yet another malignant form. This, I might add, is also inevitable absent the conviction of an alert and active *participatory democracy.*

The progressive is misanthropic by nature, despising both republicanism and capitalism primarily because he views the individual as pedestrian and divinely inspired expression as a *threat.* This *ism* considers sovereign national boundaries as archeological in nature, deriding the systemic pulse of moral virtue as pabulum for the mindless vagrant, viewing conscience as nothing more than arbitrary intercourse, malleable and interchangeable at will and thus prefers no conscience at all. This, unfortunately, is the face of contemporary American democracy.

The progressive propagates this nihilist[27] perspective not from a desire to expand and mature the human experience but from the perspective of contempt. These are the common themes that resonate through the culture of impulse driven spirit-death whose ultimate ambition is complete destruction of the human spirit by compelling, by any means necessary, complete submission to its mantra.

"TO COMPEL SUBMISSION IS TO SUPPRESS THE DISTINCTIONS OF CONSCIENCE. TO SUPPRESS THE DISTINCTIONS OF CONSCIENCE IS TO PLACE FAITH IN THE CERTAINTY OF ADVERSE CONSEQUENCE! SO THEN, WHAT BECOMES OF THE CHOICE MADE BY CONSCIENCE WHEN AMONG THE CHOICES OFFERED THERE ARE NO PROHIBITIONS?"

If we were to review the failed *isms* of history's past, we will discover the near-complete and routine absence of social conscience penetrating every level of public order, the least of which are the abstract notions of tyrannical government, its economic mode and its social mandates. The malignant regiment, equal to the task, anchored its form in the educational systems as well where the neo mind-numbing mantra was imprinted upon the *tabula rasa*, the hungry and unformed intellect of

---

27   Webster's Dictionary; Nihilism 1a: a viewpoint that traditional values and beliefs are unfounded and that existence is senseless and useless b: a doctrine that denies any objective ground of truth and especially of moral truths 2 a: a doctrine or belief that conditions in the social organization are so bad as to make destruction desirable for its own sake independent of any constructive program or possibility b: the program of a 19th century Russian party advocating revolutionary reform and using terrorism and assassination

the unsuspecting youth. Our own education system, public and private, is, with rare exception, nothing more than an efficiently automated incubator for reproductive failure.

Even to this very day, universities, tied to government funding, side with the mantra's systemic tilt for fear of losing funding while their professors, protected by tenured bias, seed the intellect of their students with the nihilist's lifeless bile. Not promoting or accelerating critical thinking but instead corrupting the mind with a toxic form of conformity mimicking the subtle message of *relativism*. Business interests, lacking financial clout, submit to Corporate Government intrusion while faith-based entities, suffering from their own version of progressive-relativism and fearing the loss of their tax-free status, quietly submit to the same intimidations.

This practice accelerated significantly under the influence of cult-like figures[28] from the '60's, the self-anointed demigods of the period who proselytized "Bring it all down, man!" to the equally misguided youths of the day. Sadly, these very same youths are now in seats of power (referred to as the "merging" above) destroying from within. A national *corporate-government* manned by relativists who have never developed the ability to think as sovereign-individual minds, uniformly functioning as an integral component of the very machinery whose sole purpose is to enforce progressive ideology, progressive anthropological and spiritual decay.

Zombie-like in their regiment, these fledglings artistically command the art of manipulation by narrowly defining the parameters of the

---

28   *Cult-like figures* such as: Timothy Leary, Ken Kesey, Ernesto Guevara, Allen Ginsberg and Saul Alinsky to name a few.

conversation intending only to conceal the depths of their culpability and the emptiness of their message. One has only to observe these characters in action to witness this emptiness first hand. Might I suggest one review the transcripts of the Secretary of the Treasury[29] or the Chairman of the Federal Reserve's[30] appearances before various Senate hearings if one is eager for a rather acute reminder.

"LET US MANUFACTURES IDEALS BASED SOLELY ON IMPULSE, NOT ON MEANS AND MOST CERTAINLY NOT ON THE SOUNDNESS OF PRINCIPLE. WE SHALL ATTIRE THE OXYMORON NOT AS A NOTION BUT AS A THOUGHTFUL CONSIDERATION AND REFER TO THESE NOBLY AS INDUCEMENTS OF TEMPTATION WHOSE PRICE OF ADMITTANCE IS THE SURRENDERING OF SOUND REASONING."

Or, as Don Miguel de Cervantes states in his novel *Don Quixote*:

> *"And so, to sum it all up, I perceive everything I say as absolutely true, and deficient in nothing whatever, and paint it all in my mind exactly as I want it to be."*

Understanding Don Quixote's rather curious form of dementia, the comment becomes a particularly appropriate metaphor for the mindlessness of the *fledgling*. Either way, when one considers that the elected contingent of the corporate government has sworn to "support and defend the Constitution," we summarily unveil a profoundly stern indictment of their actions.

---

29   Secretary of the Treasury: Timothy Geithner (January 2009 - ?)
30   Chairman of the Federal Reserve: Ben S. Bernanke (February 2006 - ?)

This cult of thought is not confined just to this country and even though the world view may choose to focus its *just* contempt upon the U.S., this is not at all a concept rooted in American republicanism. The Alliance's *divide and conquer* model of *merging* is clearly of Old World origins and, to be sure, the U.S. is fast becoming its most prolific success story. With reference to the *Three Truths* as mentioned above, the *Alliance* knows its days are limited and long ago began to seed new conquests to ease enforcement of its global ambitions. Russia narrowly escaped its clutches, at least for the time being, though the Middle East and Asia perimeter remain well within its reach.

Nonetheless, there still remains a bit of life left in the tethered American giant and after all, it sure is a lovely location for a base of operations. For token gestures of dominance under the cover of *making the world safe for democracy* and *protecting economic interests,* our ten nuclear powered aircraft carriers, complete with a powerful strike-force, come in mighty handy when the need arises. However, there is one lingering fear: There may yet remain pockets of resistance within the corporal structure that is America, so to be sure all remaining signs of viable objections are removed, the *Alliance* has a bit more plundering to perform in order to secure its perch.

What we will see, domestically, is the corporate-government move to further consolidate and expand its hold on whatever remaining freedom and economic life there might be all the while conscious of its guiding light, the indomitable *Three Truths*. They will attempt to accomplish their final assault by demonizing all things American. Domestically it will appear as *dire necessity*. Internationally their actions will be justified under the banner of a *cure for rank excess.*

"FIRST, QUIETLY AND WITH REFINED PRECISION OF A SINCERE
HAND, THE PROVOCATEUR GAINS CONFIDENCE. PENETRATING IS
THE UNSEEN HAND AS IT SEVERS THE ARTERIES WHICH CHANNEL
LIFE AND AS THE DYING LIMB FADES, THE MENACING GRIP YET
REMAINS - EAGER TO COMFORT THE FEW WHO MOURN."

A quick sidebar: I wonder if anyone other than me observes the not-so-subtle insult to the American ideal? What I am referring to is the use of the term *Czar* in the naming of presidential *special appointments*. Considering the barbarism of Czarist Russia I find its use ruthless by reference and shameful in its implications. As I'm sure you know these appointments award expansive authority to non-elected individuals completely outside the legislative process and with absolutely no congressional and judicial review – Unbelievable! However, not to worry, you're about to see the use of this *Reich Fuhrer* tactic with increased frequency. This practice is just another indication illustrating the degree of control progressives possess over political and, to a large degree as well, social issues. This organism clearly understands there is a bit more predation required in order to accomplish its most lasting and ultimate conquest; unless of course it is repelled.

THE CONQUEST OF OPTIONS:

Financial and economic control! Admittedly, accounting for the unchecked influence of private banking interests, i.e., the Federal Reserve Bank – a very effective cover, it is fair to say that domestic and to a large extent global financial control has long been established. Conquest, for this particular application has more of a global context than it does for domestic. At this juncture, frankly, I see little difference.

The financial and economic conquest is a critical move for the *Elitists* as these are the only remaining component necessary to protect and perfect their ambitions. Possessing considerable, if not complete, control of the political process these practices will continue to migrate through the financial/economic system, raiding deeply vertical and broadly horizontal[31] enterprises (large labor pools and/or those with large asset bases saddled with large debt/equity loads) such as domestic auto manufacturers on to the public services sector such as health care, energy and organic resources and then, ultimately, agriculture. In short, if it is financially vulnerable yet economically viable, it is a prime candidate.

"THE PROGRESSIVE SPEAKS HIS WILL INTO ACTION KNOWING
YOU'VE NO MEANS TO SPEAK YOUR WILL IN OPPOSITION!"

Seems unbelievable however I assure you it is not. These practices, aided by a willing media complex, create an extremely favorable environment for the *financial elite* and they do love a good media binge! An example of this type of predation is the consumption of hundreds of billions of dollars in public funds handed to banks for the purchase of so-called toxic assets. To illustrate the absurdity of this notion, i.e., purchasing toxic assets, consider the following example crafted specifically to illustrate the point:

U.S. taxpayer funds are funneled from the U.S. Treasury to purchase a defunct carburetor manufacturing company on the basis that it has

---

31   Vertical and horizontal, in this use, refers to the extent to which a business/market penetrates a given sphere of influence. GM, for example, produces/assembles (in the U.S.) a finished product the components of which are sourced from a variety of (typically) independent (domestic) enterprises. However, GM also produces/assembles a finished product in foreign locations as well. It can be argued that GM possesses both horizontal and vertical traits.

the world's largest supply of automobile carburetors (in this example, the *toxic asset*) numbering in the hundreds of thousands of units with a *notional-value* of hundreds of billions of dollars. The government experts, who themselves have beneficial interests along with the automobile industry, authenticate the proposal as a viable asset base and with the aid of politicians willing to assure the public that unless the money is spent, a crisis of epic proportions is assured and so, with no objections of conscience in attendance, your money is spent. However, there is one *massive problem* that is curiously ignored; in case you haven't heard, currently most production automobiles use fuel-injection. In short, the entire premise for the bailout is, for many reasons, flawed however what should be most obvious to one and all is that *there is no future market for an asset that has no value.* So then, one might ask: To what purpose, why use taxpayer funds to acquire an asset that has no value? A fine question with an equally refined answer: It is not the carburetors they want, it is the economic and political leverage the item and host structure assures they are after. More simply; *because they can.*

With unlimited access to seemingly unlimited funds from the Troubled Asset Relief Program (TARP), taxpayer funds are being funneled toward the purchase of mortgage instruments, in *default* status, which are then passed on to *lending/banking institutions* at severely discounted values with a guarantee to these *institutions* of as much as 90% of their original *notional-value,* plus accrued interest. Not a bad deal, unless of course you are one of the People paying for it.

Another contemporary perspective worth considering are the events surrounding the fall of the former Soviet Union: A politically and financially bankrupt system whose national resources were pillaged by hordes, both Russian and foreign interests, taking control of industrial resources and vast organic reserves. What arose, following the collapse of the corporate socialists, was only a more urbane class of economic *elite,* incrementally exercising their influence and political control to a point of refinement. If one considers, as an example, the Russian state post the collapse of the former regime, effectively what one observes is simply the refining and perfecting of the previous order one would have thought had been dismissed. Well it hasn't. It is, however, far better attired in wonderfully hand-stitched Italian suits.

From our discussions in Volume II: *Value Given, Value Received,* specifically in the chapters on *Simple Economics* and *Monetary Policy, we now understand the reasons why there will be no such functional and sustainable economic recovery through government intervention or meddling in the U.S. economy.* Absolutely none! The primary reason for the truth of this observation is captured by the PSE[32] effects of corporate government, i.e., its own life support system addressing (only) the needs of its interests! Government has not moved to address, and appears increasingly unlikely that it will, the needs of the most critical component: the nation's economic engine. The *only proven source* for functionally sustainable economic recovery is the *native economy.*[33]

To be perfectly blunt, I have absolutely no faith in the government's ability or willingness to do the obvious! Sadly, the U.S. government is, on its own, completely incapable of self-imposed restraint or self-

32   *Physio-Sociological Economics* (PSE): (From Volume II: *Value Given, Value Received*) I use this term to identify the practices and tendencies of how economic actions/events or enterprises orient themselves, intuitively, addressing or responding to sociological/political preferences or issues. The motive force is typically one of an advantage-driven response (type) form.

33   *Native economic system (native economy):* (From Volume II: *Value Given, Value Received*).The fundamental human components that when engaged require the identifier we refer to as *economy.* These human components are inseparable from and integral to a functional organic economic system and are best described as: intuitive, self-driven and a perfecting "life sustaining source" that compel demand in search of supply.

inspired regeneration and it demonstrates this functional truth on a daily basis.

"IT ONLY KNOWS MORE OF WHAT IT KNOWS AND
WHAT IT KNOWS DOES NOT INCLUDE NO!"

Unfortunately for the global movement, China, and particularly Russia, are demonstrating a willingness to say no! I realize, perhaps, that this comment may appear inflammatory however, from the vantage point of "the enemy of my enemy is my friend," the reference becomes quite provocative. I will discuss the point further in the following section, kindly rest easy for a moment more while I finish with the current topic. To that end;

It is *so* very important to understand the illusion of these various *isms* all of which manufacture the means justifying intervention. What are these means? In effect, the stirring of divisive forms of social warfare that enhance the institutional forces that enjoy the preferential result. For example: Banks love bailout-type funds particularly when they enjoy absolutely no downside risk.

I strongly encourage one to become skilled at recognizing this playbook - one of the ways of course, is to study the *Three Truths* as previously referenced. The names of the *isms* may change however, beneath the mask of seemingly legitimate ambitions lay the proven reality that they are intellectually and morally bankrupt and each ultimately doomed to failure. They profess - yet are never able to deliver upon - the altruistic dream of the unbiased distribution of social justice and political and economic resources. For a time however, the *isms* are quite effective at consolidating and controlling these ideals for the benefit of an *entitled-elite.* Using, somewhat creatively, the resource of history, we might enhance the image I intend in the following manner:

> *"As Hernando Cortez commanded, 'Burn the Ships*[34]*, we shall cut off all means and leave no living memory of liberties lost by our advances!"*

Not in this lifetime, Custer.[35] One might hope!

THE PROGRESSIVE ECONOMY

As discussed in Volume II: *Value Given, Value Received*, the U.S. economic model developed into the structure we identify as *capitalism.* We have observed and reviewed the foundations of its revolutionary thought so I'll not revisit these here but leave you with a permanent invitation to review the same should your curiosity warrant. In either case, we have also witnessed the interruption of its perfection and I fully expect it (only) to be a temporary indiscretion. I imagine an individual standing beneath the branches of an oak tree surrounded by acorns. He is distressed that there are no watermelons to be found - never mind that oak trees don't beget watermelons. It may also be of interest to consider that although attempting to propagate watermelons under the canopy of an oak tree is doomed to failure, the thought of planting his own *patch* never quite breaches the barrier that lies between entitlement and inspired effort. Conversely, I trust that enduring the frustration of

---

34   This quote is a reference to the legend of the Spanish explorer Hernando Cortez. He was believed to have ordered his men to "burn the ships" in an effort to incite a tenacious resolve, believing that if they knew there was no turning back, the crew would be compelled to insure success.

35   This reference is to Col. George Armstrong Custer and his (7th Cavalry) defeat, in June of 1876, at the Battle of Little Big Horn, also known as *Custer's Last Stand.*

doing without (watermelons) will ultimately compel the restoration of a more functional approach.

What we have now is what I will, henceforth, refer to as the *progressive economy* (PE) which I have deliberately titled with naked deference to its namesake. As was the case with *isms* of the past, we too will soon be witnessing its complete destruction for the simple reason that the PE, like our monetary policy, is functionally unsustainable. Yet, as I mentioned in the preamble to this chapter, it bears giving recognition to the form so that the soon-to-be proposed *Stimuli* will appear ever more relevant.

However, before moving forward, let us introduce a bit of levity into the conversation:

> *"'That's exactly it,' replied Don Quixote, 'that's just how beautifully I've worked it all out — because for a knight errant to go crazy for good reason, how much is that worth? My idea is to become a lunatic for no good reason at all.'"*[36]

So then, to round out the relevance of this issue, permit me the opportunity to convene a component assembly of *progressive economy* forms along with a brief description accompanying each. They are:

I. **Native Economy:** The native economy (NE) is the fundamental (historical) economic engine of this country. I include this concept by reference and purposefully so, for contrasting value. It is the very motive force and/or engine that found its roots during the time leading up to the American revolution and prospered despite the interference of the British Crown. One might even say that its

---

36   "Don Quixote" by Don Miguel de Cervantes, Part 1; 1605 and Part II: 1615

robust nature occurred and refined itself because of said interference. As presented earlier, it is the initiative of a people to assert their lawful desires by expressing the means to accommodate them and ultimately fueled by the native genius of the human spirit. In *Volume II* of this *series,* we formally defined the *native economy* as: "The fundamental human components that when engaged generate the processes we generally identify or refer to as *economy.* These *human components* are inseparable from and integral to a functional organic economic system and are best described as: intuitive, self-driven and a perfecting *life sustaining source* compelling demand in search of supply." In the instances where one hears references on the subject of the American economy, such as *durable, responsive* and/or *viable* be aware that these characterizations are due to the inherent strength of the native economy when unimpeded by or despite government intervention.

II. **Financial Economy:** The *financial economy* (FE) is purely a *speculative venture* operating and functioning only as an extension of both its covert and overt influences. The FE has evolved over the past century and despite the illusion that it is a productive and necessary function it has proven itself to be nothing more than an *institutional lottery.* The foundations on which it is based are both parasitic and counter-productive in nature. With the aid of its acquired government influence, it has taken to the perfection of its primary belief which orchestrates its own form of persistence through the crafting of its own ideals. Here are just a few examples:

1. Harvesting of wealth through the elimination of the most productive component of an economy; the *productive-class* (also offensively referred to as the *middle-class*).

2. Speculative and predatory financial ventures, foreign and domestic, in lieu of expanding and/or further developing the *native economy.*

3. The strategic use of government resources for the express purpose of assuring the preceding two items.

The FE has reconstituted proven *wealth-creating* principles in such a manner as to void the functional ideals that not only sustain a productive and vibrant economy but also those practices that cause it to continuously expand. It has replaced these functional practices with a series of *insolvent-truths* the notions of which have been thoroughly integrated. What has emerged is the leviathan of *corporate-governance* and the pandemic of systemic speculation both of which have squandered our once-sacred republican heritage and our nation's honor.

One should also understand exactly what the term *market* means in the FE. Financial markets, as they function in the FE, are not *value-added* enterprises. They are neither purveyors of nor creators of capital but function only as *wealth-consumers* of capital. Doubt me? Well then, attempt to find any individual who can identify the location of the $1,144 trillion[37] ($1.144 quadrillion) of capital supposedly created by derivatives? For those who, during the 2006-2009 time period, sustained 50% plus losses in your retirement/investment plan, if you didn't spend it, is it unreasonable for one to consider where it went?

---

37   Bank of International Settlements, Basel, Switzerland

By-the-by, do consider that the global GDP (2008) is just barely above the $60 trillion mark. In other words, do not trouble yourself wondering where exactly the $1.144 quadrillion might be, not unlike the equity in your home or retirement fund, simply stated, it doesn't exist. In actuality, not unlike the currency in your pocket, wallet or bank account, if it existed at all, it was only on paper.

For the folks who espouse acquiring gold as an *inflation-hedge,* ask yourself one very simple question: When was the last time you went to the grocery store and bought a loaf of bread with a nugget or a cold coin? You should know that using gold as a medium of exchange is illegal in the U.S. Only legal tender or legal specie which, ironically, has *no intrinsic value whatsoever,* may be exchanged in commerce. Interesting!

The FE, in form, is best characterized by its similarity to its invertebrate cousin, the parasite. In practice, its resolve and expansive impact is most surprisingly similar to that of a swarm of locusts. This overindulgent and near insatiable appetite is accommodated, submissively, by the ever-present, willing and compliant political über-structure.

If one were to create an anecdotal reference for the FE as practiced, it might be expressed in this way:

"IT IS NOTHING MORE THAN A BLACK HOLE LOOKING FOR A NICHE TO FILL. A DESIRE LOOKING FOR ONES DESIRE IT CAN DESIRE!"

III. **Entitlement Economy:** The *entitlement economy* (EE) is the *hybrid economic institution.* It is, in fact, the *Corporate Government's* manufactured economy. It is the complete opposite of a *free market* concept and the sworn predator of the *native economy.* The EE is sustained by conscripting the *native economy's* productive forces. What funding it is unable to extort from the *native economy* it obtains from the *financial economy* and its *modus operandi* is completely asymmetrical in every form and is best defined as:

"WE MANUFACTURE SOLUTIONS FOR PROBLEMS WE'VE CREATED!"

Understanding that the EE occurs by the abstract merging of influences of or from the *financial economy,* one may observe its methodology in its most conspicuous form which in practice becomes;

"NOTHING MORE THAN PLAYGROUND POLITICS, PLACING DISCRETION IN THE HANDS OF THE UNINFORMED WHO HAVE BECOME MISINFORMED BY THE MAL-INFORMED!"

Government, as the supreme creator of *entitlement,* has become a form of political blood-sport demonstrating elementary school-like machinations. In practice, it attempts inconspicuous maneuvers intended not to *out* maneuver but *over* maneuver an opposing or competing position and in so doing quickly matures into the ultimate exhibition and practice of *flat-earth idolatry* (FEI). The entire operation manufactures a structure enabling its enforcement and then ultimately preserves its form by restricting access to its precisely defined yet universally flexible interpretation of its processes. After all, when you can define what is appropriate for your action or function, should an objection surface, one simply redefines the form to suitably mitigate the problem. EE is, as it speaks for itself, an idea that uses its constructed paradigm to manipulate its defense mechanisms by professing, as an absolute, what is only an illusion. Example: The People are entitled to free health care.

Ultimately, all *idolatries* collapse under the weight of a belief that is foundationally superior. This of course is my hope, otherwise, our footing is far shakier then I could have ever imagined.

PROGRESSIVE ECONOMIC CONSEQUENCE:

For all of its Orwellian-like[38] effort, what then is the product of such inspired genius, that is, the much-touted nirvana of *progressive-economics?* Well, from all indications and likely prognostications, not much. In short, I'm of the opinion, and I know I'm not the only one in the club, that *progressive economics* (PE) was, is and will always be an apocalyptic failure. As in the case with our nation's monetary policy, its functional purpose exists only in the domain of the *conceptual.* In practice, *progressive economics* is completely unsustainable and matures only as an accelerant; similar in form to using two opposing flame-throwers for burning a candle at both ends.

In either case, before moving on to our suggestions for a Functional Stimulus, let us consume a few final moments and retire to the theatre for a front row viewing of a short-film entitled, *The Play of Consequence.* The scenes are laden with a conspicuous blight whose cause lies squarely at the feet of a government's complete abdication of its duty. Kindly reacquaint yourself with a comment from Volume I: *We Hold These Truths*:

---

38   The use of the word "Orwellian" refers to the various political and social conditions detrimental to a society based on the principles of justice and freedom all of which are characterized in George Orwell's novel *Nineteen Eighty-Four*. As in the case of Huxley's *Brave New World* and Ayn Rand's *Atlas Shrugged*, if you have not read them, I strongly recommend that you do. In the case of *Atlas Shrugged*, to be frank, yes I do have issues with the Objectivists theory; however, both the John Galt *radio-speech* and the Francisco d'Anconia *money-speech* are so well written, they alone are worth the price of admission.

"THE PEOPLE'S GREATEST TORMENT IS NEITHER FEAR NOR THE ABANDONMENT OF THEIR MORAL COMPASS. NO, IT IS MORE LIKELY THAT IT IS THEIR SENSE OF DUTY AND HONOR THAT HAS BEEN CORRUPTED BY THE COMPLETE AND UTTER DISBELIEF THAT THEIR OWN HAVE SO WILLINGLY AND SO RECKLESSLY VIOLATED THEIR TRUST!"

To control the length and breadth of this section I trust you will indulge me a modicum of literary license. I have come to realize that the topics, political and economic, are intertwined to such a degree that it is seemingly impossible for me to come up with a means to weave them in to a manageable dialogue. To that end, what follows, in truly no particular order, is a select and limited series of personal observations; I trust the significance of each do not suffer at the hand of my rather peculiar method of presentation.

Grateful as I am for your accommodation, do consider the following commentaries. I readily admit they are at times painfully detailed; however, if your desire is as mine to find a way forward, we must first grasp the significance of the obstacles which we will all need to overcome.[39]

---

39   Note to the reader: Many of these observations may only be relevant thru June 2009 time period. I acknowledge that events may either mitigate my concerns; though, to be quite frank, it is more likely the case that events will only cause further aggravation.

"ONE OF OUR GREATEST CHALLENGES TO OVERCOME
WILL BE THAT WHILE IN A POSITION OF LEADERSHIP WE
HAVE NOT PLANNED, PRACTICED OR PERFECTED A SELF-
PERPETUATING SYSTEM FOR INSURING A FUTURE EQUAL TO
OUR OWN PROMISE. WHETHER IN OUR VALUE OF LIFE, OUR
PRACTICES OF FAITH, INDUSTRY OR GOVERNANCE, WE HAVE
SQUANDERED OUR ADVANTAGES IN NEARLY EVERY AREA
AND IN THEIR PLACE WE HAVE SUBSTITUTED BELLIGERENT
INDIFFERENCE AND THE PERFECTED ART OF PLUNDERING."

1. Economic Health Indicators (EHI): These *indicators* are the equivalent of frogs to the health status of an ecosystem, all indicating
   severe economic decline. It is far too causal an economic observation to look only at finished goods, inventory or manufacturing
   outputs to recite a conclusive outlook or commentary. The reason
   for this, which may not be obvious, is that these statistics are less
   than insightful as they often represent end product or refined results and thus not true indicators or measures of systemic wealth
   creation or capacity. Far too often economic statistics, such as in
   the case of Gross Domestic Product (GDP), indicating growth or
   expansion are typically the result of inflationary forces, increases in
   government spending or both.

   Also, as to systemic (domestic) health, there is little value in statistical information for offshore-sourced output. For instance, one
   may value his flat panel television, the components and assembly
   of which occur in Asia; however your acquisition of this product is
   a *wealth consumption multiplier.* For example: (a) This acquisition
   consumes your wealth. (b) The importing of the product contributes to a trade imbalance. (c) There is the loss of domestic jobs

in the assembly and component sourcing process as well as the various economic losses sustained absent the vertical and horizontal flow of revenues generated from the entire process occurring in a domestic environment.

Needless to say, there is also the issue of suppressed wages due to increased unemployment. The aggregate losses occurring system-wide are often overlooked as well. For example: Increased government deficit (debt) spending to make up for loss of government revenues and loss of technical and manufacturing skills to name but a few. Multiply these effects by the number of market segments such as textiles, transportation, agriculture, energy, medical, electronics and so on one can quickly determine the extent to which and the reasons for our bleak economic outlook.

Never accept the notion that *service-based* economies, public or private, can prosper in an environment where they are a *net* and *aggregate consumer of wealth.* To illustrate my initial point, let me present just one of many authentic indicators: "The total U.S. market for machine tools in January 2009 was $95 million, a decline of 72 percent from the same month in 2008 when sales were at $338 million, according to Association for Manufacturing Technology.[40]" From this one statistic, the reduction in machine tools sales, we can extract several EHI's, among these include: (1) Contraction in domestic manufacturing output. (2) Contraction in raw material production. (3) Reduction in sales revenues. (4) Reduction in corporate tax liability. (5) Reduction in payroll. (6) Reduction in sales tax revenues. (7) Increased unemployment.

---

40   "Manufacturing & Technology News", March 31, 2009, Vo16, No. 5

(8) Increased demand for unemployment benefits. (9) Decreased demand for industry support services. And so on.

What one should observe from this example is the exponential effect of a system's practice of *failed economic policies*. With each step along the chain, the width and depth of the impact both widen and deepen, dramatically. If one were also to consider other such EHI's such as foundry output, perishable and durable goods output, each segment indicates an economic outlook that is moving well beyond *life-support* capabilities.

2.   Gold: Perhaps with the exception of crude oil or currency arbitrage, there is no more effective tool for controlling currency volume/flow than gold. The orchestration of the commodity markets accommodates this outcome by consuming vast amounts of currency at the point of purchase (particularly useful when the market responds to the *inflation-hedge* motivation). The gold markets are likely to be less erratic than one would otherwise expect due in large part to the commercial use of gold. Yet, the impulse nature of speculative *market-response* still makes for an incredibly volatile exchange and one that is equally vulnerable to the *swings* inherent with these types of markets.

> "RARE IS THE CASE TO FIND A NON-MARKET-INSIDER PROFITING ON THE INFLATION-HEDGE HYPE; HOWEVER, COMMON IS THE OCCURRENCE OF THE INSIDER RECORDING MASSIVE GAINS ON THEIR LOSSES."

In an era where the liberal creation of government debt is used to address massive deficit spending, unfunded entitlement demands such as in the case of Social Security/Medicaid-Medicare, as well as the numerous *bailouts*; gold markets become increasingly volatile and all too often quite deliberately so. One of the consequent observations resolves then to the following: It is not so much that investors are drawn to gold as a hedge but more so that the available options appear far more perilous. Emphasis on the word *appear.*

Unsettling as the previous observation may be, there is one additional thought that might stir one's curiosity: Central banks, such as the Federal Reserve Bank, are known to use a rather complex gold bullion trading schemes to control currency values. This, in very simple terms, occurs when the central bank *leases* a nation's gold to a *bullion bank market maker* such as JP Morgan-Chase or HSBC. Entities such as these actively participate in the global gold commodities market, trading various derivative–like instruments which they also originate. So much for the *hedge* concept.

For further discussion on this topic I will refer you to page 93 of Volume II: *Value Given, Value Received* and the chapter entitled "The Dangers of Fiat Money." Very interesting observations.

3.   Control by Depravity: As we observe the U.S. economic environment over the last quarter century, one can easily see the effects of the *conjoined global economic concept.* It is much easier to manipulate a population through the use of controlled economic depravity, the hungry and desperate are far more malleable. In a socio-economic structure such as the United States the notion of *depravity* is used to turn The People and their ideals in opposition to one another and ultimately to further and expanded dependence on government. Whereas independent social and econom-

ic structures produce positive tension, both social and economic, directing The People away from government dependence and toward self-reliance.

The conflict within our boarders is the result of a *manufactured-identity.* What people identify as the Democrat and/or Republican parties; as somehow being the mandated attributions of Republicanism; are not components of Republicanism at all. We, as a People, must understand that these are complete illusions manufactured and employed to facilitate the use of government for purposes inconsistent with one's sovereign and unalienable rights. What people are now awakening to is the maturation of a divisive process seeded long ago. Nonetheless, it is destroying our relationships with one another through the *selective-indifference* of an extraordinarily *unfaithful companion*: Partisan Politics.

4. Global Impositions: Global economic/monetary systems institutionalize sclerotic economic policy. A global stagnation where resources, human or otherwise, are apportioned to meet a specified outcome. Planned economies have proven their systemic flaw time and time again the root cause of which is that they are entirely void of *creative impulse* and the *breadth of beneficial rewards.* The *globalist,* as with all regimes, configures itself to appeal to the *brooding civilian* who has been cultured to think of him or herself as *disadvantaged.* These become the soldiers of change who goose-step in formation armed with the banner-of-the-day proclamation whether it be totalitarian, imperialist, eco-conscience or simple nihilist in nature. These formations become magnetic for those who are unwilling or unable to stand, as a source of personal identity, on the conviction of independent and sovereign nobil-

ity. Unfortunately, the mindless find comfort only in the *village of conformity.*

The *globalist* uses these organisms to effect change and does so with rapier-like efficiency practiced and refined over centuries. The independent minded are far too often unaware of these migrations until the *imposition of insolvent-truths* threaten these sovereign individualists with the very bindings to which the *villagers* so willingly surrendered.

5. Financial Markets: Beginning in the second quarter of 2008 there has been a conspicuous increase in the frequency in conversations on the subject of financial market liquidity. I am of the opinion that what is actually occurring is not at all an issue of market liquidity. More likely what is occurring *is* the convergence of delusional dysfunction with its committed opponent, functional reality. It is important to consider that the financial system is based on the *fiat money concept* which we discussed thoroughly in Volume II of the *Series.* Understanding this reality, how then can one find soundness in a statement that makes the claim that there is a liquidity problem? Or is this statement simply a cover for some *thing* else? Is it possible that what we see playing out before us is the mathematical impossibility (discussed in Volume II: *Value Given, Value Received*) of the *progressive economic model?* Or, is it that what we are witnessing is nothing more than a calculated move (*manufactured-crisis*) to further destabilize The People for the express purpose of easing the progressive's global transformation agenda? Just a simple question one might be inclined to consider.

If there is truly a lack of liquidity in the market then where are the *dollars* coming from to shore up/support the Treasury (bond) market? What and who is supporting the over-valued stock market and why? What is the source of the massive capital flow (in U.S. dollars) purchasing sovereign-debt of certain European-Union member nations? This is the *lottery* of the speculative and manipulated markets and an example of why using gold as a hedge is so nonproductive. Now, if gold were useable as specie or physically traded, then my statement could become, under certain circumstances, inaccurate. However, as it is not, this gives us reason to consider precisely why my statement is sustainable. It is entirely possible that the money going into the market is coming from the various bailout/stimulus packages and/or from the Federal Reserve directly.

Only a complete fool or accomplice will choose to ignore what is otherwise so completely obvious. I truly believe that the stage is being set for a complete and total *nuclear approach* to the current financial/monetary system. The crisis that this will create, if not averted, will be the calling card for global financial control managed by the dominant entity of global governance, which has long been the goal of global financial interests. The 17th century financier Mayer A. Rothschild's words were appropriately used in Volume II; they are equally so in this instance:

> "LET ME ISSUE AND CONTROL A NATION'S MONEY
> AND I CARE NOT WHO WRITES THE LAWS."

The call for a global solution to the financial crisis is creeping into the daily conversation. With no exception and for reasons previously discussed, the dream of global financial control under the banner of totalitarian utopian conformity *will never work.*

However, this doesn't mean that yet another attempt at failure will not occur. The progressive ideology of the *entitled elite know best*, evidenced by the current state of affairs, has well documented its folly.

<blockquote>
"THE URGE TO SAVE HUMANITY IS ALMOST ALWAYS A FALSE FRONT FOR THE URGE TO RULE."[41]
</blockquote>

6. Toxic Brew: The mix of economics and politics begets a *toxic brew*. The fact of the matter is that very few politicians have the faculties necessary to comprehend conjoined concepts and are far too vulnerable to the bias of economic and financial influences. Example: Note a prominent New York Senator's comments following the passage of the *Financial Services Modernization Act of 1999*. "If we don't pass this bill, we could find London or Frankfurt or years down the road Shanghai becoming the financial capital of the world… There are many reasons for this bill, but first and foremost is to ensure that U.S. financial firms remain competitive."[42] Competitive indeed!

7. Speculative Collusion: In the glossy self-indulgent world of the PE, so-called *markets* exist only to create profit from the transaction and not from the productive nature of the underlying commodity. These *markets* are (only) the physical extension of the *fiat money* and *fractional-reserve banking* (which on its own also operates much like a fiat money system) systems which in like-kind exist only to create ways of evolving a transaction base (financial

---

41   Henry Louis Mencken (1880-1956) – American satirist and journalist.

42   The New York Times: "Congress Passes Wide-Ranging Bill Easing Bank Laws," by: Stephen Labaton, November 5, 1999

opportunities and instruments) creating both profit and economic influence simultaneously. This fundamental reality is both the reason why *banking* needs to be confined to the function of banking and not permitted access to the *speculative financial services investment market* (SFSIM). What we should have learned, once again, from witnessing yet another implosion of the so-called *financial markets* is the inevitability of assured destruction when there is collusion between banking, policy (politics) and SFSIM's. This collusion is why the markets are so easily manipulated and when accompanied by an *uncontrolled monetary policy*, precisely why they are both so destructive and incredibly volatile.

8. Budgeting Dysfunction: Here are a few numbers that I find very interesting and so should you: (a) Proposed U.S. 2010 fiscal year budget is $3.55 trillion dollars,[43] which, it should be noted, does not include the sundries covered by the numerous off-budget items. (b) As of April 30, 2009, "The government has made commitments of about $12.2 trillion and spent $2.5 trillion…"[44] as part of its interventionist approach to managing the U.S. economy. Note that these amounts do not include the $700 billion TARP adventure nor, at the time of this writing, the $3+ trillion the Federal Reserve, in 2009 alone, has distributed outside both the legislative process and the U.S. borders. (c) The "Social Security and Medicare Trustees Reports" (2009 Report) indicates that the combined liability, unfunded, of these two programs has reached nearly $107 trillion in today's dollars. (d) The U.S. Treasury (5/09) reports that the total U.S. government debt at $11.4

---

43   U.S. Government: OMB

44   The New York Times - "Bailout Tab" 2/3/09. Alternate Source: Treasury; Federal Reserve; Federal Deposit Insurance Corporation.

trillion, not including the approximate $412 billion (U.S. Treasury, 2008 budget) in annual debt service costs and the commitments mentioned in item (b) above.

Note: Consider that all of these cost projections ignore the consequences of further tax revenue losses due to further economic decline. As the national economy continues to contract, so will tax revenues – *at all levels of government* – serving to further increase both government deficit spending demands and the unfunded exposure of entitlement programs. More to the point, by my own calculations from figures obtained from federal government sources, if the present decline in federal tax revenues continues at the current rate, by June 2010, both illusory projections of Social Security trust fund and Medicaid/Medicare solvency will have vaporized.

If one is not entirely clear at this point as to how far out of near-earth orbit the *progressive ideologue* has traveled then consider a few interesting tidbits of information: (a) The total U.S. gross domestic product (GDP), which includes government spending, is (only) in the $14 trillion range. (b) Using the Federal Reserve's own figures (5/09), the total notional value of global U.S. "Money Stock" (M2) is reported to be $8.3 trillion. And (c) The total government exposure, from our numbers in the preceding paragraph, excluding however, the *unknowns* such as off-budget items, including but not limited to ongoing Middle East incursion costs, U.N. mandates, proposed and future bailouts/stimulus, derivatives exposure, unfunded defense contracts, the yet unresolved issue of the various health care proposals, which, from my own calculation, by 2015 will add unfunded costs of nearly $872 billion per year, etc. - *appears completely unimaginable at $140 trillion* not including annual debt service costs! Reminder once again, the U.S. GDP is $14 trillion and this number includes government spending.

Is *anyone* paying attention? I'm at a loss to explain the mindset of an individual who would link his future to the sinking ship that is *progressive politics* and the rather peculiar economic science that bears that name. Stimulus packages, bailouts, toxic assets and now health care! We might consider that the best description for this unique approach to economic life-support be referred to as: *Pagan-Economics.*

9.   Derivatives: The size of the derivatives bubble, according to the *Bank for International Settlements in Basel, Switzerland,*[45] is esti-mated as of 12/07 at 1.144 quadrillion or $1,144 trillion dollars. Estimating the global population at six billion people, that is nearly $190k per person. However, looking at the statistics now available from fourth quarter 2008, the numbers appear to have significant-ly worsened – BIS has suspended releasing summary information.

Derivatives are securities whose value depends on the underlying value of other basic securities and associated risks. They include the better-known instruments we know as futures, options and various other over-the-counter instruments such as interest rate swaps, foreign currency and interest rates contracts, commodities and various equity instruments. Derivatives are the near-perfect image of what best illustrates the progressive's Financial Economy (FE) described above. Truly, *"It is nothing more than a black hole*

---

45   Bank for International Settlements: website: www.bis.org

looking for a niche to fill. A desire looking for one's desire it can desire!" The perfected enterprise enabling the locust unlimited access to the machinery that manufactures fields for plunder.

10. Institutionalized Failure: The pilotless drone of *progressive economics,* it would appear, is likely to make its pass over the manufactured healthcare crisis. As if the mega-failure of the government-run *all you can eat* approach to institutionalized entitlement programs isn't sufficient cause for prohibitions of conscience, we're about to see the same methods and practices responsible for the resounding success of programs such as Social Security, Medicaid and Medicare applied with equal and universal efficiency.[46] Yes, sarcasm intended.

As in the case of morality and intellect, it is not possible for government to legislate economic efficiency. In point of fact, whether it be military procurements or for that matter any government function or program that results in monetary expenditures, government is incapable of the concept of economic efficiencies for the simple reason that this feature is only *a resident function of the positive tensions native to free market forces*. Governments, as most definitely is the case with the U.S., possess no such market intuitive forces; accordingly, their legislative blank check has - and equally so - no such imposition. It spends and fouls at will. Consider just one of government's many systemic approaches to economic efficiency: Medicare Part D, which prohibits negotiating competitive pricing on pharmaceuticals. Who needs market forces when an entire industry can legislate its own demand?

---

46   For reference purposes, I would direct my readership to page 59 of Volume II: Value Given, Value Received and the dissertation relating to Government Entitlement Projections and the accuracy of the Congressional Budget Office (see footnote #23 therein).

The notion of national health care is yet another illustration of how government, having distorted the marketplace, creates yet another illusion inviting further intrusion. A specific example of this is where health care providers, wanting to weed out the non-profitable segments of their risk base, create the idea of the *uninsured*. Progressivism welcomes the invitation for the *manufactured crisis* and provides the concept of Medicaid/Medicare as well as other state sponsored health programs, e.g., California's Medi-Cal program, all of which enable and give form to the *uninsured* concept. Simply brilliant!

As in the case of industries that create toxic waste, unwilling to assume the expense of cleanup, craft a crisis of ecological disaster giving life to taxpayer supplied *Superfunds*. Insurance companies, not wanting to honor the claims promised by their policies, create the crisis that calls for *tort reform*. High-risk segments of the population, unwilling to accept the costs associated with their lifestyles, choices or age groups, have converged and now are known by the progressive ideologues as the *entitled uninsured*. As is the case with all forms of *pagan-economics*, the politician, insurance and medical industry - all looking for a good band wagon - seize upon the opportunity with the inevitable result being the one-cure-fits-all single payer notion of yet another entitlement. After all, why create a cure when you can create a crisis?[47]

11. <u>Health Care Costs</u>: Why are US health care costs so high? Here are a few examples and underlying each one should apply the element

---

47   For reference purposes, I would direct my readership to page 61 of Volume II: Value Given, Value Received and the dissertation relating to government economics, Systemic Cost Multiplier Effect, Physio-Sociological Economics and Tortional Economic Forces (be sure to view the related footnotes therein).

of certainty. Certainty that it is directly related to government intervention: (1) Excessive administrative costs due to lack of standardization and bureaucratic inefficiencies. (2) Pharmaceutical industry bias has increased drug costs. This is directly related to consumer advertising that encourages the use of expensive drugs. Prohibitions in federal programs that forbid price competition and, likely, a patent system that prohibits the competitive advantage of generic drugs. (3) Current structure discourages personal responsibility for individual health maintenance and discourages prohibitions against high risk behaviors. (4) Reimbursement for basic procedures that should be borne by the individual. (5) The advent of defensive medicine practices have increased costs. Physicians are forced to make medical decisions always with exposure costs in mind in lieu of the interests of sound medical practice. For years the absence of limits (caps) on lawsuits has driven many physicians out of practice. (6) The excessive costs in ER and ICU care. This is particularly relevant to the issue of indigent and illegals' care among the many causal forces that place an unmanageable cost burden on the health care system. And by no means less significant are the costs associated with *end-of-life* issues which include the futility of *do-everything* practices. (7) No cap/limits on seniors' health care, where incredibly expensive surgeries are performed on 80-100 year olds where, on issues of sound practices, the surgeries would never take place. (8) To combat the systemic problem and related administrative costs of medical history management, we should consider a portable card-like devise that electronically stores medical history and insurance information. Alternatively, a uniform electronic system maintained by the primary care provider. (9) Inmate health care costs which routinely provide 100% reimbursement for all care: hip replacement, joint replacement and cases where indigents suffering from "withdrawals" - pursuant to the curiously manufactured *Alcohol Protocol* which deals with the effects of DT's (a government mandate) - will actually arrange to get arrested in order to receive free *meds*. From my own contacts in the medical fields, I have learned that there are (many) actual cases of individuals engaging in unlawful acts simply to be arrested in order to receive needed surgeries. (10) The cost shifting practices whereby various government programs shift unreimbursed costs of entitlement care to the private health care sector. These are a few of the many that came to mind.

12. Successful Failure: Observing the Wal-Mart business model is an extraordinary opportunity for viewing the impact of *progressive economics* on the *native economy*. For instance, "more than 70 per cent of the commodities"[48] sold in Wal-Mart are imports from China. My comments are not intended to assail Wal-Mart or its approach to prospering in its market environment; nonetheless, the observation is unavoidable when considering the operational consequence, as it is, from the practices of *progressive economics*.

Progressive economics does not promote economic excellence through market forces, it attempts instead to persist only by default. In the absence of competition, there is no shopping for the lowest price or best value, in reality, there is only the supply that is made available. Accordingly, as is often the case with *progressive economics*, *successful failure* is championed as a desired outcome. How then is this a truly compelling indicator of success? After all,

---

48   "Wal-Mart's China inventory to hit US$18b this year." By Jiang Jingjing (China Business Weekly) Updated: 2004-11-29 15:21

"WHEN THE BAR IS SET SUFFICIENTLY LOW, EVEN
MEDIOCRITY CAN MEASURE SUCCESS!"

There is no substantiated data securing the argument that labor costs in the U.S. justify the exporting of an entire industrial base. Particularly when we consider the costs of unemployment, the loss of the productive benefit associated with a sustainable economy and the cumulative financial burden. The aggregate cost of these rip through the entire national economy with the force and effect of a tsunami. However, on the issue of trade with China, the following information is quite an affirmation: "The 2.4 million jobs lost/workers displaced nationwide since 2001 are distributed among all 50 states, the District of Columbia, and Puerto Rico, with the biggest losers, in numeric terms: California (370,000 jobs), Texas (193,700), New York (140,500), Illinois (105,500), Florida (101,600), Pennsylvania (95,700), North Carolina (95,100), Ohio (91,800), Georgia (78,100), and Massachusetts (72,800).[49]

The economic costs to this nation tower in comparison to whatever possible advantage the labor cost argument might tender. Looking at the Wal-Mart model as the most conspicuous example of *progressive economics,* I believe one can observe the "locust" metaphor in action. These practices have nearly obliterated the vibrant nature of the *native economy.*

13. Efficient Policy: As a companion to the aforementioned, consider the percentage of people, in the top 10 major U.S. cities, living below the poverty level. This is absolutely shameful and for any

49   Economic Policy Institute: "Unfair China Trade Costs Local Jobs" - Robert E. Scott, March 23, 2010

who witness a comment on so called *global free trade* and its dynamic benefits, I trust you will consider the efficiency of this policy when considering the following: "Detroit, Michigan: 32.5%, Buffalo, New York: 29.9%, Cincinnati, Ohio: 27.8%, Miami, Florida: 26.9%, St. Louis, Missouri: 26.8%, El Paso, Texas: 26.4%, Milwaukee, Wisconsin: 26.2%, Philadelphia, Pennsylvania: 25.1% and, Newark, New Jersey: 24.2%."[50] These are the promised results of *progressive economics.*

14. <u>The Cycle of Predation</u>: PE has surrendered U.S. economic might in return for foraging rights. In so doing, we have exported domestic *wealth creating* forces which will only add to our exponentially increasing government debt and contribute further to the nation's stunning losses in GDP. To feed the beast of *progressive economics,* the *cycle of predation* must be continued. This is the truth that lies behind globalism.

The government attempts to offset trade deficits and curtail the growing absenteeism (at Treasury auctions) of foreign investors by turning over ownership of U.S. assets to foreign or global control. Unfortunately for the nation, this practice serves only to further direct the flow of *wealth creating* forces away from Americans and on to foreign interests. For the U.S., this practice is the economic equivalent of the Germans having signed the Treaty of Versailles. The government's response has been to suggest that we can resolve the productive losses to the U.S. economy by retraining the unemployed for the *economy of the future.* Yes indeed, your future, their economy.

50   U.S. Census Bureau: American Community Survey, 2006, August 2007.

The opposition argument will contend that these comments suggest a return toward *isolationism*. The mere suggestion of this notion is to illustrate the depths of the mal-informed. Would one suggest that a solider - by virtue of his purpose - equipping himself with a rifle and thus having done so is now deemed an isolationist? Of course not!

> "ISOLATIONISM IS NEVER AN INTENDED CHOICE; IT IS HOWEVER ALWAYS THE CONSPICUOUS FUNCTION OF IMPOSITION THREATENED BY AN EXTERNAL FORCE!"

15. Economic Overdosing: The PE's approach has been to cure the patient by overdosing. Massive deficit spending, massive monetization of debt by the Federal Reserve and massive new debt issuances by the U.S. Treasury. This approach is pushing the dollar, as a *world reserve currency*, to the breach of oblivion. In nearly every critical economic segment, save possibly for agriculture, this nation has become an import resource-dependent country. In the case of agriculture, I use the word *possibly* from the perspective that as of 2005, the U.S. for the first time in 50 years, became a net importer of food. We can thank the genius of the U.S. Senate for their faithful support of U.S. sovereignty by their passage of the WTO/GATT, NAFTA and CAFTA trade agreements.

If, as it appears increasingly possible, the U.S. loses its *reserve currency status*, it will not be able to pay for these imports as foreign exporters will no longer be willing to accept payments in U.S. denominations. Preventative measures, one of which is to increase interest rates to attract investors, frequently prove to be a double-edged sword in *fiat* money systems. Interest hikes, in circumstances such as we find presently, often yield further economic contractions and release abrupt inflationary pressures. Further, similar in nature to the economic environment that gave rise to the collapse of Thailand's currency in 1997, the U.S. dollar might further suffer form aggressive currency speculation the result of which will be no different for the U.S. than as it was for Thailand. A derivatives implosion might very well have the same effect.

It is only a matter of time before the emerging economies discover they have no need for the IMF or the U.S. currency (No Value = No Demand). Should they discover the simplicity of available alternatives, they will rapidly move away from the current approach (U.S. dollar as *reserve currency)*. It would seem perfectly reasonable that a sovereign nation should want to control its economic destiny; however, any attempt at projecting sovereign interests, as we can clearly observe in the United States, will result in the classic approach: a *manufactured crisis,* an *emerging opportunity* or both.

Whatever the invitation, the expeditionary force will be lead by U.S. and Old World financial interests that will likely mandate the imposition of a replacement global currency system administered by or under the cover of the International Monetary Fund (IMF) or the United Nations (now there's a contradiction in terms) and rest assured, it will be divisive and woeful in effect.

Why will this happen? Simply this: the U.S. and Old World interests will not surrender their global financial grip to the principles of sound fiscal discipline. Financial interests have never been opposed to tossing the youth of America into the fray of *gunboat* diplomacy.

In the practice of government as it is, the only effective opposition is an abundance of courage, discipline and principle-based discernment. To be sincere, I see no evidence that persons bearing these traits will or can be sourced from within the ranks of the current regime. Political or financial.

16. Reckless Financial Practices: According to the report "Sold Out: How Wall Street and Washington Betrayed America," published in March 2009 by the *Consumer Education Foundation,* the financial sector, from 1998 through 2008, invested more than "…$5 billion in political influence-purchasing in Washington over the past decade, with as many as 3,000 lobbyists winning deregulation and other policy decisions that led directly to the current financial collapse."

    According to the report "Sold Out: How Wall Street and Washington Betrayed America," published in March 2009 by the Consumer Education Foundation, the financial sector, from…

    Repealing the rigors of the 1933 Glass-Segal Act and replacing the same with the PE's version of financial management, The Financial Services Modernization Act of 1999 and the Commodities Futures Modernization Act of 2000, were the rewards congress handed the financial sector. Where once there existed at least the appearance of prohibitions against reckless financial practices, the flood gates were now open courtesy of well-placed financial lubricants. Government regulators were equally at fault by turning a near complete blind-eye to even the most egregious and conspicuous abuses.

Being no stranger to the influences of the financial sector, let us consider a few interesting political appointments: two former chairman of Goldman Sachs, Robert Rubin and Henry Paulson, have held the position of U.S. Treasury Secretary. Laurence Summers, Director of the National Economic Council, was the managing director of D.E. Shaw, one of the largest hedge funds in the world. In November of 1999 following the passage of *The Financial Services Modernization Act of 1999,* Summers stated, "Today, congress voted to update the rules that have governed financial services since the great depression and replace them with a system for the 21st Century. This historic legislation will better enable American companies to compete in the new economy." The fox built the hen house, anesthetized the hens and then proceeded to self-regulated access. How nice.

Michael Froman, Deputy National Security Advisor for International Economic Affairs, is himself a former Citigroup executive. And of course, we have Mr. Geithner, who has migrated through various Wall Street financial institutions, influential advisory-groups, political appointments, President of the Federal Reserve Bank of New York, and now, not surprisingly, the U.S. Treasury Secretary.

It is safe to consider that there is no such thing as political or economic coincidence. For this and for many other reasons, the temptations of Wall Street influence, being far too strong a bias, should be sufficient cause to bar any member of this community from ever being granted a *chair* at this level of government.

17. <u>Subrogation</u>: As the *wealth creating* economic concept (*native economy*) has been increasingly subrogated by *progressive econom-*

ics, the most conspicuous consequences of this conversion and the most severe are directly felt by individual Americans. *Progressive economics* has the double-edged effect of both depressing household incomes and increasing wealth consumption. The net effect of this is that households are forced into their own form of deficit spending - evidenced by the historically high levels of debt accumulation by/in the *household sector*.

Reviewing household use of home equity as a source of purchasing power yields information wholly consistent with the previous observation: (1) "During the 1991-2005 period, free cash resulting from the three types of equity extraction averaged about $530 billion annually. Equity extracted through sales of existing homes accounted for about two-thirds of total free cash; home equity loans accounted for close to 20 percent, and cash-out refinancings."[51] (2) "According to our estimates, an average of $60 billion per year of home equity loans (15 percent of total HE debt outstanding at the beginning of the year) was repaid as a result of home sales and the refinancing of first liens during the 1991-2005 period."[52] (3) "Equity extraction was used to repay an average of about $50 billion of non-mortgage consumer debt per year from 1991 to 2005...."[53] And, (4) "An estimated $164 billion per year of equity extraction was used to acquire assets...."[54] The sum of these transaction amounts to over $4 trillion in debt-cycling,

51   Finance and Economics Discussion Series Divisions of Research and Statistics and Monetary Affairs: Federal Reserve Board, Washington, D.C.: Sources and Uses of Equity Extracted from Homes, 2007: Alan Greenspan and James Kennedy

52   ibid

53   ibid

54   ibid

and this occurred within one (household) segment of the U.S. economy, all within a five-year period.

By no coincidence, these indicators closely mirror the accelerated transitions of *progressive economics*. More interesting is to consider one other rather intriguing parallel: Is there a connection between the free-fall in consumer spending and the fact that the banks have universally suspended the practice of offering home equity lines of credit (HELOCS)? The facts are unassailable; the connection is undeniable.

18. The Under Reporting of Failure: United States Department of Labor[55] places the national unemployment rate at 9.7%. However upon closer inspection of the Bureau of Labor Statistics and expanding their sample to include those that "…were not counted as unemployed because they had not searched for work in the 4 weeks preceding the survey,"[56] the number is actually 13.7%.

Let us extend the inquiry a bit further to include the government figures in their totality: "…the stated unemployed, the unemployed who are in temporary low paying part-time jobs and those who have given up looking…." then the actual number is closer to 18.3! California, by comparison, Employment Development Department (EDD), on March 26th, 2010, released the state's unemployment rate at 12.5%. Considering that the EDD models unemployment in a fashion similar to the USBLS (using the base published rate of 9.7%) it is more likely that the California rate is closer to 17%. By comparison, the EDD archives place the historically most reliable rate (highest) at 14.7% (October of 1940).

---

55   USDL/BLS Economic New Release: "Employment Situation Summary" dated 4/2/10.

56   ibid

Conspicuously absent from these numbers are the unemployment rates of the following: The self-employed (although technically occupied by a trade or business) who are generating little or no net income, the self-employed who are unemployed due to business closures and finally those who, either self-employed or as principals of a corporate business or partnership interest have - evidenced by bankruptcy filings - business failures. Recall, of course, that few if any, self-employed have or receive unemployment benefits from the federal or state governments.

The Small Business Administration (SBA) trend reporting indicates a stunning increase in loan failures: in 2004 the reported failure rate was 2.4%; by the fiscal year ending September 2009 the most current information we were able to confirm the rate was nearly 12%.

"Bankruptcy filings in February 2010 continued at a steady level: the total filings were about 112,000, up slightly from 103,000 in January, but down from 114,000 in December. Because February filings normally are 10-15% higher than January filings, the slight increase is not significant. On a year-to-date basis, filings in January and February of this year are 14% higher than the same time a year ago. To put that in context, filings last summer were more than 30% higher than the previous year's filings."[57]

What I trust my readership will glean from this information is not only the utter failure of government mismanaged economic policy, particularly as to underutilization of our productive labor

---

57   National Bankruptcy Research Center - February 2010 Bankruptcy Filings Report

resources, but the extent to which the government relies on *the practice of under-reporting to conceal its perfecting of systemic failure.*

In truth, the unemployment rate in the form and manner reported is, in many ways, meaningless. However it should be clear, from a deeper review and consideration of the statistical information, that we should resolve to the need for an entirely new conceptual measure: The measure of *productive employment* as a more precise measure of labor force utilization. Taking into account the flaws within the existing format as well as the measured effects discussed, then I would proffer that our *productive unemployment rate* is closer to 35%[58], if not more.

Last point: Using the government's reporting assumption it is not at all unreasonable to expect that unemployment, statistically, will likely trend downward. Why? Sooner or later there will be so few jobs from which the People can become unemployed that once the "four week" survey period passes, these underemployed will no longer be included in the calculation. We can then conclude that having fewer and fewer jobs from which to measure unemployment, inevitably, the rate will fall. The government bureaucracies will have 100% employment and the private sector (no longer having anyone to fire or lay-off) will as well. Remember, when you make the rules, you also define precisely how and if they apply.

These commentaries would not be complete if I failed to address the culpability of corporate America (CA) and its significant part in the destruction of the American ideal. I do not fault their sub-

---

58   Admittedly a light calculation (it is likely much higher) using U.S.B.L.S. unreported unemployment figures (see footnote #57) Bankruptcy number from footnote #59 reference and the Small Business Administration "failure rates".

scription to capitalism in fact, I am one of capitalism's many supporters. I do fault *corporate America's* lack of intuitive foresight and resolute regard for the American ideals that made their fabulous success possible. Were it up to me, I would strip them of their ill-gotten gains and imprison their political enablers as a warning to others tempted by similar ambitions.

This organism's practice of trading profitability for political influence produced the bastard-child of republicanism that continues to soil our sovereign national heritage; yes, partisan politics. Instead of posting gains from and adapting resources to domestic technological innovation, they sought speculative gain in financial schemes both domestically and on foreign shores. Where developing a productive, dynamic and adaptable corporate ideology offering the perpetual bounty of productivity could have been the option selected, genius was instead, sequestered in favor of mediocrity and *elitist* boardroom doctrine. When confronted with the imposition of *collective-bargaining*, productive capacity was surrendered to *progressivism's* arbitrary and derelict notions of *social-justice*.

However, to me the worst and most tragic action of all was and is their defiling of that which has, historically, been most sacred and precious; the organic basis of trust and faith that binds the ideals which ultimately define America. To suggest that these are the mere actions of the so-called *rich* is to oversimplify the causal forces and thus ignore the culpability of the uninspired and predatory grunion whose actions are enabled by the lack of opposition. Whatever the case, one fact remains unassailable: The price of consequence is universally applied. Shame, shame on the lot of you; banker, businessman and politician alike.

These are but a few of the *progressive-economic* theories that are housed within the concocted school of thought I refer to as *paganomics*. I must confess however that more and more I am drawn to an updated reference, a replacement term for this collection of theories. For some reason, *Obamanomics* seems more appropriate.

"THERE IS NO AVOIDING CONSEQUENCE. THERE IS ONLY FACING ITS RAGE WITH THE RESOLVE OF FOCUSED AND DISCIPLINED ACTION. HE WHO IS MOST CULPABLE WILL SOUND THE SEVEREST OF OBJECTIONS."

A Functional Stimulus

"THE SUM OF WHAT HAS COME BEFORE
DELIVERS ONE YET ANOTHER CHOICE!"

CONSIDERATIONS:

TO THIS POINT, we have been companions through this literary journey and having been so, the following suggestions will come as no surprise. They are, as I intended, the ultimate resolution upon which the entire Blind Vision series was constructed. To be sure, the *stimulus concepts* (SC) that follow are by no means an exhaustive essay on every possible solution nor will they target every possible permutation of cumulative disorder; they are deliberate as to purpose yet conceptually fluid so as to be supremely and universally adaptable.

Upon thoughtful consideration, I trust the readership will find each extraordinary in its intended focus and collateral benefit, but most importantly, even the most casual observation will find each wholly consistent with the ambition of both political and economic recovery with a stern allegiance to our nation's republican ideals. At their core rest the very fundamentals discussed in *We Hold These Truths* and *Value Given, Value Received* and each inexorably bound to that which we hold to be *self-evident!*

"OF LIBERTY I WOULD SAY THAT, IN THE WHOLE PLENITUDE OF ITS EXTENT, IT IS UNOBSTRUCTED ACTION ACCORDING TO OUR WILL. BUT RIGHTFUL LIBERTY IS UNOBSTRUCTED ACTION ACCORDING TO OUR WILL WITHIN LIMITS DRAWN AROUND US BY THE EQUAL RIGHTS OF OTHERS. I DO NOT ADD 'WITHIN THE LIMITS OF THE LAW,' BECAUSE LAW IS OFTEN BUT THE TYRANT'S WILL, AND ALWAYS SO WHEN IT VIOLATES THE RIGHT OF AN INDIVIDUAL."[59]

I intend that the totality of what follows be considered as a course of travel conspiring with a desire to fulfill the promise of "We hold these truths to be self-evident, that all Men are Created Equal…" and I encourage each of you to consider them with a measured degree of deliberation.

Aware as I am of the complex task of unwinding the cumulative effects of mindless government, I am ever more faithful in the vast reserves of diligent resolve should we choose to mount a campaign aimed at delivering, in our time, on said promise. The idea has never lost its universal virtue and is as equal in its importance today as it was for the Founding Fathers on July 4th, 1776. So much so, they signed the Declaration of Independence with a testament of extraordinary resolve:

"…FOR THE SUPPORT OF THIS DECLARATION, WITH A FIRM RELIANCE ON THE PROTECTION OF DIVINE PROVIDENCE, WE MUTUALLY PLEDGE TO EACH OTHER OUR LIVES, OUR FORTUNES AND OUR SACRED HONOR."

In this testament we witness unity and supreme accountability in purpose and though the Founding Fathers were clearly of different

---

59   Thomas Jefferson to Isaac H. Tiffany, 1819

minds, they did persist and speak as if one voice. Who among us will demonstrate the same courage? If our intentions are to honor the sacrifices of those who have come before us, courage will be the bond that perfects our ambitions.

I believe it so very important to recall and recall again and again the following point which is integral to the *concepts* that soon follow: Politics is not *good governance*. Despite the suggestion of necessity, it is the mask worn by the annelid that penetrates the skin, the parasite that thrives off the host that is *good government*. There are only two possible evolutions of government; (A) one which prohibits the parasitic nature of political machinations and its numerous variations or (B), one which morphs in response to these intrusions and succumbs to the inevitability of unsustainable burden and ultimate collapse.

The Supreme Creator defines perfect structure then initiating action to create form, that is, form follows structure. He operates from the regiment of structure and expands upon the same again and again yet the form of the creative process remains resolute, systematic, precise; both changing as it relates to the *progenerative-process* and simultaneously unchanging as to the structure upon which the process is based. Man too, in much the same way, must operate within this very same structure and void tendencies to act or function in spite of it. *Injustices, of all kinds, are the direct result of violating this basic tenet.*

Precise direction produces a precision response; imprecise (wayward) direction produces only an undefined result – this is the law of consequence in a nut-shell. Everything is possible but anything may not be appropriately so; we often refer to these as unintended consequences. So then, to conclude the point:

"IT'S NOT SUFFICIENT TO KNOW YOUR SHIP IS SINKING, IT'S MORE IMPORTANT TO SURVIVE IN ORDER TO BUILD A BETTER SHIP!"

A FUNCTIONAL STIMULUS DEFINED:

Over the last few years the overuse of the word *change* has, ironically, seemingly forever altered the meaning of the word. Where once, in its most common use, its simplest implication was nothing more than to *change one's shoes, to change one's direction from north to south* or *the change in one's pocket.* In contemporary parlance, post the 2008 presidential election cycle, it has come to mean something quite different. *Change* now has an entirely new cover, *a metaphor* if you will, that is its own form of *subversive entitlement - enabling license* and now defined as follows: *To alter, to redefine, to reinterpret, to radically transform.*

With this metaphor in mind I trust that when I suggest that we need to change the *discussion about* and the *purpose of what* it means to be an American from that of a political process or orientation to one that evolves from the ideal, i.e., the best practices of freedom's pursuit, my readership will be equally transformed with an entirely new sense of *urgency.*

Regardless of one's affinity for these propositions, I trust they will inspire meaningful thought, discourse and ultimately, considered and deliberate action. As you read through and study each, remember this: There is no fixing the system as it is, the dysfunction of government as it is practiced *will not allow it.* There is only excising the malignant forms as they are and restoring the structure from the *radically transformed* to that which was *defined as its purpose.*

"I BELIEVE THAT OUR GREATEST CHALLENGE WILL BE
OVERCOMING THE RISK OF DEFINING THE DISCUSSION AS
BEING A CHOICE AMONG COMPETING POLITICAL IDEOLOGIES
WHEN THE ISSUE AT HAND IS FAR GREATER. THIS NATION
FINDS ITSELF AT A DEFINING MOMENT ALONG THE PATH
TOWARD AN UNCERTAIN FUTURE; THE COURSE WE SELECT
WILL BE SEEN BY FUTURE GENERATIONS AS EITHER INSPIRED
OR TRAGICALLY PREDICTABLE. AS THEN GENERAL GEORGE
WASHINGTON SAID IN 1783, 'HAD THIS DAY BEEN WANTING,
THE WORLD HAD NEVER SEEN THE LAST STAGE OF PERFECTION
TO WHICH HUMAN NATURE IS CAPABLE OF ATTAINING.'"

IF WE DO NOT RALLY around a common theme, a common and specifically defined declaration, then developing independent campaigns
such as the Tea Party movement will be easily derailed by strategically
placed operatives who will define for themselves what becomes of both
your movements and your ambitions. Case in point: Consider the
influence the independent movement *United We Stand America* had
once Ross Perot strategically withdrew from the 1996 presidential
campaign. What became of those whose ambitions for preserving
freedom and liberty no longer had a voice? I'll leave the answer to your
discerning efforts.

My contributions, in scheduled format and with accompanying
comments, are as follows:

STIMULUS CONCEPT 1: **RECONSTITUTION**

The following bullets represent *primers,* issues broad in scope, which will be developed further throughout the various *concepts* that follow:

- We must review and remedy the flaws in our election process. Representative government functions only when representative of the *public will.*

- We must begin to champion the ideal of *self-reliance* in ourselves and national economy all the while working to restore the practice of accountability and moral authority in our individual actions.

- We must begin to champion a *culture of life* and void the contamination of the human spirit where and whenever possible.

- We must begin to champion not only *grace and charity* with one another, but first with ourselves.

- We must begin to champion a *commitment to lifelong learning and productivity.*

- We must *rethink* the concept of *retirement.* We have adapted to false expectations based upon theories that are not only impractical but equally unsustainable in their resource and deliverability.

- We must begin to champion the connection of *applied effort* with *earned reward* and void the temptation of *entitlement* and *government-sponsored reliance.*

- We must remind ourselves *never to suffer in silence* at the hand of a tyrant. Ever.

- We must restore the sanctuary concept of *day of rest*. We need to turn ourselves *off* and spend this time in *personal perfecting* and *reflection*. Here's an idea, sit on your front porch and visit with your neighbors and discuss life's great questions. If you don't have a porch, sit on your sidewalk, driveway or hallway and make a point to not just make eye-contact, *make heart and mind contact.*

However one interprets these initial *primers,* one must use caution not to misinterpret their intent. It would be wholly inappropriate to believe that the intent is to confine your choice to what you may perceive that each implies; rather, it is that you have the right to perceive them as you choose. Their purpose is to provide context and to encourage a universal desire to insure the framework by resolving to be a nation *converging upon* and *projecting from* a common ideal and not the maneuverings of a few.

> "NOT A VILLAGE OF THE MINDLESS BUT INSTEAD, A LEGION OF INDIVIDUALS WILLING TO AROUSE, INTUITIVELY, WHAT IS MOST RIGHTEOUS AT THEIR CORE SO THAT EACH IS FREE TO EXPRESS HIS OR HER CHOICE WITHIN SUCH BOUNDARIES SO AS TO VOID IMPOSITIONS UPON THE FREE EXPRESSIONS OF ANOTHER."

Rest assured, you will need to make a choice and as you will discover, it will be the same two options from which your choice will be made: *Freedom* or *Tyranny.*

If the choice is to insist on and enforce self-government (republican-ism) then *We the People* must *reconstitute* a national intention to do just that. If it is to be so, it will start with one choice and one voice, one at a time *Standing4* what is common to all.

Strange as it may seem, I have no dislike for progressive-socialists; perhaps somewhere along the way something happened that distorted their life-view, a Christmas gift wish went unfilled, a third grade classmate teased them for eating paste or they discovered that they were never going to be able to sing like Ray Charles. Who truly knows for sure? Whatever the reason, they've concocted a view that, in effect, suggests they've evolved to an *entitled higher life form.* It may likely be that progressive-socialist believe that their intellectual prowess is sustained by the measure of selectively recorded success. Still we must not ignore the pathology of progressivism, the measure of its cumula-tive damage is undeniable and its thallic-like theology is unsustainable; if for this reason only, it must be dismissed with great prejudice. In either case, humor aside, legions of Americans are simply and sternly opposed to their *ism* particularly as it violates a fundamental precept of American Ideology - *sovereign rights.*

If you believe, truly believe in the ideals that are the foundation of this nation then you cannot, must not, be anything other than an American, regardless of what part of the globe you reside. We must come to insist that it be no other *thing* than that: Not Irish-American, Italian-American, African-American, Mexican-American, and so on. This does not mean to surrender one's heritage, absolutely not, the color of our individual customs adds to the on-canvas splendor that gives brilliance and definition to our People. So then, if we intend to pull forward, then we must pull in the same direction; "…in purpose and though the Founding Fathers were clearly of different minds, they did however persist and speak as if one voice!" *Different minds, speaking with one voice!*

Our greatest success is yet to come and it will be found in our individual, governmental and economic restoration. Just as Mr. Jefferson said it would, 200 plus years ago!

> *"The tree of liberty must be refreshed from time to time with the blood of patriots and tyrants."*[60]

STIMULUS CONCEPT 2: **ELECTION PROCESS**

Suspend the Electoral College system. Its abuse by the two-party system, which James Madison expressed concern over in Federalist No.10, has rendered it irretrievably biased and self-serving. Unless and until the present two-party system is deconstructed, this process will never resolve to its intended form.

- Establish secure citizen-voter registration system with a six-month pre-election cutoff. Election fraud has become nothing more than a secret ballot mechanism and must be eliminated. This can be as simple as a citizenship code-identifier embedded in a state-issued driver's license or I.D. card.

- Eliminate campaign financial assistance of any kind. The infiltration of unchecked and unregulated influence has contaminated the public will with the structural distortions of financial bias.

60   Thomas Jefferson

- Establish a public campaign outlet using the Public Broadcasting System (PBS). This concept supports the cleansing intentions offered by the previous *concept*.

- Establish a *4/2 Month Campaign Rule*. Mandate a not-to-exceed four month campaign cycle. The process might consist exclusively of traditional signage and electronic web-based mechanisms followed by, in the last two months, *live* dedicated and relevant issue-based discourse via PBS outlets. Far too much time and resources are wasted in the process where only programmed discussion and scripted responses are projected. The People are entitled to meaningful, relevant, transparent and unscripted discourse.

- Qualifying presidential candidates may not simultaneously hold elected office and campaign for the highest office of the land. Fraternal government associations have proven themselves far too damaging to the intended and un-biased nature of republicanism. Furthermore, an elected official should busy themselves with the functions of their office for the benefit of The People who elected them to office and not be dismissive of this duty by seeking further and expanded conquest.

- Qualifying presidential candidates, prior to announcing their candidacy, must submit to a thorough security and background check. I was surprised to discover that such was not the case.

- Promote and establish a Non-Partisan Constitutional Party. As we've discussed, the existing two-party system will not reform itself; its very existence is proof of its contempt for constitutional directives. Thus being the case, the only way to restore representative government – which by now you should know does not exist – will be to vote in a representative party that will dismantle this systemic blight. We truly need to break the hold partisan politics has on the process. There will have to be a functional alternative available to The People in order to perfect a desirable outcome. How can we claim to be a representative democracy when fully two thirds of the potential voting public is not represented by the party in power?

- Establish online public reporting data illustrating both the entire text of proposed legislation, 30 days in advance (save for national emergencies), as well as a candidate's legislative history and voting practices where a history exists. This function will, as well, need to indicate whether the elected official actually read the proposed legislation prior to casting their vote. There has to be some form of accountability, presently, there is none.

- Establish overlapping two-term limits for all elected offices (federal, state and local). Career government has proven to be unmanageable and the legislative process needs to be brought under control. The notion of the seasoned politician is the functional equivalent of the seasoned alcoholic. The president has term limits, and so should congress. The concept of overlapping is to avoid concurrent office transitions by state.

- Contemporary politics thrives on divisiveness and disintegration. It is the preferred method in their procedural manual: *How to Win Elections When You've Nothing to Offer!*

"AS A NATION, WE WILL THRIVE ON VIBRANT AND PASSIONATE DISCOURSE BUT WE WILL NEVER RESOLVE ON DISCORD."

There is a choice that will most assuredly have to be made, either by you The People or by a *force* that will define what your choice will be. It is a very simple process with *powerful* consequences: Are we to claim our birthright of self-government or submit to its destruction? There is no middle ground, there is no soft-socialism and there is no *gentle tyranny.*

Throughout the body of this work I have presented several examples and metaphors for the nature and means of tyrannical government, most recently via the *Three Truths* (see section entitled: *Systemic Realities).* There is no mistaking the realities of present day government and its detachment from all things functional. Like all self-induced excesses, they become known by their power-hungry addictions and conspicuous by their indifference to the representative process and the public will. Their divisiveness has become so extreme as to no loner be inseparable from their own perceptions and their practices. They have, as we can see by the regard the public holds for their performance (if only to consider the U.S. Congress[61]), gone *completely rogue.*

Recently I was called upon to answer a question that asked: "In your opinion, what is the single greatest cause for the government's dysfunction?" In summation of my response, I opined that the problem

---

61   CBS News Opinion Poll : 3/29-4/1/10 places Congressional Disapproval Ratings at 74%, 10% "unsure".

(likely) rests solely on the issue of *money politics* as it should come as no surprise that money buys influence. Unfortunately, the influence is always biased and always disproportionate to the interests of those who possess no such means. Government influence, not unlike the acquisition of any advocate, whether economic or political, *is a transaction of convenience* and is always the cause of disproportionate result and disparity in/of resources. The very nature of the transaction, particularly in the practice of government, is to endorse the practice of select representation and this is not the life-blood of republicanism, it is its rival! Any suggestion of "it's a necessary evil" is ultimately rooted in a biased and/or self-serving motive.

Government will not be willing to execute self-imposed restraint and therefore the only apparent means will be to install a structure that can defeat or exhaust its tendencies. To that end, The People's only true option is to establish an alternate party whereby consistent and focused effort is applied to sufficiently populate the congress with those representatives willing to reestablish the *representative* process.

The more immediate approach is to court voting blocks much as a candidate, in exchange for money or endorsement, assures seniors' groups and various unions of his allegiance. This idea gives rise to a rather interesting question: Is it possible, in exchange for an endorsement, to bind a politician to a performance contract so that should he or she morph into yet another political stooge an entity might sue for *specific performance* or *damages?* Clearly taking an oath to "defend and protected the constitution" appears sufficiently inadequate to compel allegiance; perhaps what the People need is a more punitive and immediate device?

Whatever the choice, the approach will have to be done with lightning-like speed and with as little warning as possible; otherwise, the existing system will move to enact prohibitions barring such an attempt. At the very least, it will seal every possible access point, which in effect, yields the same result.

"THE CURRENT POLITICAL SYSTEM HAS CONVINCED ITSELF
AND MUCH OF THE PUBLIC THAT ACCESS TO THE HALLS OF
GOVERNMENT MUST AND CAN ONLY OCCUR WITH THEIR CONSENT.
TO DENOUNCE THEIR HOLD ON THE PROCESS, IN THEIR VIEW,
IS TANTAMOUNT TO HERESY AND SEDITIOUS IN NATURE."

As discussed in a previous volume, it is important to note that the two-party system of partisan politics is a completely manufactured concept and has never been a practice consistent with our form of government. The current practice of Democrat or Republican Party rule creates nothing more than voting blocks where any legislative action is marked only by its party affiliation and typically resolves along said party lines. Institutionalizing bias is not representative government and I believe its existence is grotesquely unjust, a national embarrassment and supremely unfaithful to the republican ideal of our founding charter.[62]

---

62   Update: (3/29/10) This paragraph is acutely relevant when considering the effects of the recently passed Health Care Reform Bill. Rasmussen (3/21/10) Poll indicates only a 26% public approval of the Bill yet with Democratic control the executive and legislative branches of government, it passed non-the-less. A perfect example of party-block politics in action: In this form of democracy, who represents the unrepresented? I am sure James Madison and (even) John Adams are most distressed; this is not at all what they envisioned.

STIMULUS CONCEPT 3:
MONETARY/BANKING POLICY

- Eliminate all autonomous actions of the Federal Reserve Bank. No entity should have the ability to bind, negotiate or transact on behalf of the U.S. government with impunity and without the advise and consent of the congress.

- Restore monetary policy as a function of the U.S. government. Private ownership and maintenance of a national monetary system is, by its very nature, divisive and well proven to be a significant contributor to economic dysfunction. Absorb only the beneficial and functional administrative resources of the Fed into a *monetary management system* not unlike that which is proposed in *Value Given, Value Received*'s section on Monetary Policy.

- Strongly consider the establishment of a Domestic Currency to be issued directly by the U.S. Treasury. This *currency* would have few conspicuous differences and issued in similar denominations as is the present practice and would be specifically limited in both volume and purpose: either for government infrastructure improvements or for residual funding for eliminated government entitlements as suggested in SC-7 below. This *D-Currency* will be administered only by the U.S. Treasury and though it may be absorbed into the existing banking system there must be a distinct accounting, domestic-only circulation and not considered part of reserve requirement mandates for conventional banks and credit unions. The currency circulation volume will be tied to the notional value of a hybrid portfolio of silver bullion and 30-year D-C Bonds, which will bear, tax free, a nominal rate of interest not to exceed 3.75%. These D-C Bonds will be made available for purchase, directly from the U.S. Treasury. The proceeds might be used to fund either or both a *national home mortgage fund* providing qualified borrowers 30-year fully amortized financing at a rate 1.5% above the nominal rate and/or infrastructure improvements. The two primary purposes of this concept are: (1) To suspend the domestic loss, by the People, of their wealth due to inflation. (2) To fracture the influences of international banking interests and to draw capital away from speculative non-wealth creating ventures.

- Strictly define the practices of banking. The nature of money (the lubricant of commerce) is always at risk of contracting economic vice. Money has no conscience and accordingly will only accompany the course on or to which it is directed. Accordingly, the function of banking should be strictly confined to a precisely defined domain and with strictly enforced and end elevated reserve requirements. Among the specificity enumerated prohibitions: insurance, securities origination and securities trading, derivative origination and trading, commodity trading, and currency speculation, to name a few. Notice, I didn't say these practices are prohibited. They are, however, off limits to the business and practice of banking.

- Eliminate all free market interventions by government. Free flow of capital is important to a vibrant economic climate;

however, these forces, which seek to maximize economic result, function efficiently only under the tension of an open market format. Regulations should exist only to enforce transparent disclosure and to observe and report abuses for severely punitive judicial action, with no exception. The current state of the financial and securities markets is due primarily to the fact that the only participants who make money in the speculative ventures are those who define the rules of its operation – more and more, the astute investor and general public are arriving at the same conclusion. If there is no faith in the form and its structure, it will not function faithfully.

- Impose a permanent *no pay no pass* requirement upon government spending. Save for national emergency declaration by both houses of congress, the practice of deficit spending must, once and for all, be brought to an end. If the government's only means of funding legislation is based solely on its ability to tax or to leverage the People's future, the legislation may not be considered. We must come to a point where we intuitively grasp the concept of *the cost of government* both in economic and social terms.

"WITH EACH NEW DAY WE MUST AFFIRM OUR
TRUST IN ONE ANOTHER. WE DO THIS BY
RE-EARNING IT WITH EACH NEW EFFORT."

This nation must rethink its monetary/banking policy concepts. The private banking concept of the Federal Reserve bank has been in place for nearly 100 years! The track record is clear; the scars on our economic landscape are blinding in their conspicuous form - I believe the Federal Reserve has had ample opportunity to prove its worth and to the extent it has attempted validation, it has proven itself a dismal failure!

As much as I like the academic idea of a precious metal standard, the systemic risks of the idea in practice, I fear, make its use far too vulnerable to abuses. However, I strongly support a national policy of maintaining a progressively expanding gold reserve as a means, among others, to hypothecate financial settlements of/in international trade and possibly in support of D-Currency and D-C Bond concepts mentioned above, as applicable to SC 7 below and as more fully discussed in *Monetary Policy* in Volume II of this Series.

If we are going to persist with the central bank philosophy then that is all the more reason why it should be confined to the function of banking. As well, if we persist with the fiat money concept, then it cannot be permitted exposure to the systemic nature of speculative risk and must only ever (fiat money) *be permitted in volumes equal to our national economy's actual productive output.* Otherwise, the nation will continue to be susceptible to *Obamanomic*-style life-support systems which mean bailouts, more and more bailouts and government confiscation of private property and industry.

After-the-fact regulation is the knee-jerk response of fools-governance and the People know a duck and cover move when they see it. The truth that lies behind the government's motivation for flooding various outlets with trillions upon trillions of dollars can be seen in a dark room. In the parlance of the day, "it is what it is" and what it is can be explained by this simple statement: *the progressive's ruse is to conceal the inefficiencies and abuses of the system they'd rather not address or otherwise acknowledge their complicity.*

Regardless, with the multiplier effect of market forces producing the inevitable and transient pandemic that is the evolved culture of speculative markets (Oh Dear Lord, I just found myself sounding like Alan Greenspan!), the inherent risks need to be announced and made clear to the investor. *If you can't afford to lose, then you cannot afford to play.* If you lose in the market it should be your own money that is wasted, not The People's. To that end, any regulating of the markets has to include and insist that both the risk management and disclosure functions be brought in to the regulative and enforcement function. And, to be clear, if the punitive penalties for violating the rules are sufficiently severe and uniformly applied then perhaps we might yet encourage a more risk-sensitive culture amongst the banking and financial practitioners. We might even consider reviewing a series of suggested concepts with Mr. Milken.

STIMULUS CONCEPT 4: **LEGISLATIVE**

- *Line item veto.* To be sure, neither the executive nor the legislative branches like the idea. It places too conspicuous a burden upon their sanctuary which is why the few attempts at enacting this tool have always failed. The system, continuously, needs to be made to work as intended. In representative government, the only *sacred item* is the U.S. Constitution.

- *Enact legislation* to permanently ban lobbyists and all political action committees. In the age of near instant information resources, elected officials, with the aid of their staffs, should review and evaluate the needs of their constituents on the functional standing of an issue. Lobbyists are only the wicked cousin of the same pandemic risks associated with current campaign finance practices. Who speaks for those who have no well-financed and vocal lobby?

• *Rescind all* economic assistance and trade agreements. As part of the concept discussed below (SC-8) and with consideration to the devastating effects these agreements have imposed on the U.S. economic landscape, there is no choice but to reverse the source of said impositions. The only trade agreements crafted must preserve and respect economic sovereignty and promote economic vitality. Those agreements meeting this (former) condition must have a government revenue generating feature – there must be value placed on the privilege of gaining access to these shores. The U.S. economy must never again be burdened with political indifference in pursuit of or in exchange for the political influence of a foreign nation.

• *Establish prohibitions* on unfunded mandates, earmarks, legislative riders, and require identification of the sponsoring/recipient parties as well as complete descriptions of beneficial enticements. The slight of hand practice of inserting mandates, earmarks, and riders has become a well-refined skill masterfully executed in the *pay-to-play* pandemic of government corruption. The cleverest occur within the House Appropriations Committee where the process has evolved to be nothing more than a last minute clearing-house for political favoritism. I would also suggest that should partisan practices persist, there should – at the minimum – be a mandate that prohibits majority-party legislators from *chairing* any committee or leadership position. Understanding, as I do, that it is not functionally possible to remove the Constitutional provision known as the *power of the purse,* still by instituting many of the concepts from SC-2 as well as other *current light of day* transparencies we might yet hope to impose a measure of discipline upon a process that presently has absolutely none.

- *Restore sound* monetary/banking policies. Refer both to SC-3 above and the section "Monetary Policy," in Volume II of this series, *Value Given, Value Received.*

- *Suspend or repeal* all international treaties and/or agreements subordinating Constitutional or sovereign authority to any entity, for any reason, other than as specified by the Constitution of the United Sates of America. The reasons for this, by now, should be obvious.

- *Construct a mechanism* for controlling immigration policy. For the many reasons discussed in Volume I: *We Hold These Truths,* specifically those in the section entitled *Immigration,* there can be no such thing as uncontrolled entry, legal or otherwise. Any proposed legislation, to be meaningful, must include English-only provisions, criminal record prohibitions, health, education and financial or employment requirements, a citizen and public benefits waiting period of no less than five years as well as correcting the misinterpretation of the 14th Amendment, the so-called *anchor baby* loophole. It must also state that if a person, any person, is in the country illegally, he or she is immediately ineligible for citizenship for a period of no less than five years. The unresolved issue of immigration is a price this nation can no longer afford. Disintegration must not be permitted to exist in this nation if we hope to speak with one voice. We must promote and assert that there is *value in America*; we do this by delivering on and protecting its promise.

- *Suspend collective bargaining statutes.* This is not to suggest that unions may not have a place in the American economic system; I am however, suggesting that they should not have government sponsorship of any kind. If there is value in *union affiliation* then let that be sufficient cause to compel one's participation. Mandating membership as a condition of employment violates several fundamental and implied sover- eign and Constitutional rights, the most relevant of which is the free exchange of one's property – end of story. Further, to burden the economic model with undue influence of political and economic bias is a form of *restraint of trade*. Establishing the concept of forced bargaining has enabled a political blockade both in the private and public sectors of the economy. Specifically in the case of public unions, the aggravated costs of forced bargaining has produced public benefits that are well beyond those available to the public who, it is important to note, ultimately funds these benefits.

- *Restore all prohibitions relating to* public advertising of phar- maceuticals. This contributes to impulse-driven medical and pharmaceutical industry biases and is a major contributor to ballooning medical costs. Why, when the political-speak of the day rails against protectionist policies do we allow the pharmaceutical industry to conspicuously parade its exemption?

- *Require all legislation* to specifically state all enabling parameters. Far too often legislation is enacted leaving the most critical components to bureaucratic interpretation, development and enforcement. Often, as in the case with the EPA, the bureaucracy is given license, *ex post facto*, to create both the domain and content of the statutes as well as their methods of enforcement. On the state and local levels as well this same form of license gives rise to wildly invasive regulations from land use and zoning regulations to selective use of car-pool lanes. Legislative actions should never provide unlimited and open-ended license to regulate.

- *Pursue action that promotes* the ideals of all eight Stimulus Concepts. This will require the function of sound governance whereby existing laws will have to be completely rescinded or legislation passed to silence them. It must be the practice of government to honor the Constitution not by reinventing it but through the practice of extolling its virtues and ideals. A fine platform from which to start a *true independent reform movement.*

- *Reactivate states' rights.* Each state in the union will need to take a more aggressive stance with the federal government by insisting on *cutting the ties that BUY!* State government has become both co-dependent and accomplice in the migration away from the principles of self-government. The People have a far better chance of reconstituting the federal government if we can win an alliance with our own state governors and legislatures. Partisan politicking, at the state level, is a far more accessible target than the detached bastions of Washington, D.C.

- *Limit Congressional session,* on an annual basis, to no more than six two-week sessions each occurring every other month. If we are unable to, at first, restore the process, perhaps we can interrupt the damage it leaves behind.

I readily admit, as I've often said, I possess little hope for the government to willingly take on any of these Concepts. I do however have great faith in The People mounting an effective campaign to enforce their will. Government at its best should have an equalizing effect on national policy, unfortunately government in excess, as we have witnessed and as is practiced, operates only as a destabilizing influence. It has come to be a force that distorts the playing field by selectively altering the bar to benefit a designated few and we, as a People, have far too long endured the lowering of this bar and each of these Concepts is directed at reversing this trend.

Government action has never stimulated economic health; at best, it suppresses its required motivations. Government believes it stirs economic expansion by burdening the economic system with massive debt. This practice, in its various forms, saddles the economy first with a program's initial costs and then the systemic costs of managing the program and finally, the ongoing and expanding nature of the debt and interest costs to pay for it.

If these costs weren't sufficient to make the point, then consider the untold costs associated with lost economic opportunity consumed by the non-productive nature of the programs. In short, not only do these programs not create wealth, they progressively and systemically consume it! Feel free to review the many examples illustrated throughout this *Series* in addition to the dizzying array of federal and state programs; however, here is one particularly prototypical example: *Social Security.*

We must restore the idea that any legislation must be economically self-sustaining. Otherwise, the blank-check practices of *pagan-economics* will persist along with the financial burden and economic turmoil continuously passing on from one generation to the next.

The *line item veto* is a must! In concert with the *light of day concepts* mentioned above, the *line item veto* is necessary to permit conspicuous expressions of conscientious opposition and the means to observe these practices when they occur. Now this is transparency, Mr. President!

STIMULUS CONCEPT 5: **JUDICIAL**

- *Presidential oversight.* Presidential actions have increasingly demonstrated a terrifying willingness on the part of the executive branch to establish wholly autonomous practices that appear to traverse well beyond the boundaries of *Constitutional authority.* No president should ever have a right not expressly defined by the Constitution or granted to this branch expressly by The People. Where, once again, is the U.S. Supreme Court?

- *Congressional oversight.* Likewise, in the case of congress, the legislative practices have moved well beyond the delusional confines of a drug-induced stupor! Both houses continue to expand the legislative boundaries beyond every known limit with ever-increasing conscriptions of freedom and resources. Again, where is the U.S. Supreme Court?

The doors of the executive and legislative branches of government appear to have been closed to The People and unless one has the temerity of a militant derelict or the financial resources of the Federal Reserve, expect no response. That leaves the judicial branch as the lone representative of The People's Constitutionally protected rights.

Why is the U.S. Supreme Court so dispassionate? Why do these select few, the final arbiters of the U.S. Constitution, remain strangely absent from the process of protecting our nation's doctrine from the travesties of injustice? Who protects the Constitution when both the executive and legislative branches are intoxicated with a dismissive sense unto The People? How does one explain the intrusion of The People's sovereign rights in the face of legislation such as the Patriot Act, or United Nation and World Court mandates?

<u>Well, I have a solution</u>: A *U.S. Supreme Court Constitutional Oversight Board* whose sole function is to provide strict commentary and scoring on the constitutionality of all proposed legislation and presidential actions including executive orders. The Court will, within 30 days of a congressional or presidential action/order, issue its commentaries in a form not at all dissimilar to its present practice of issuing decisions.

Depending on the outcome, i.e., scoring, the legislative action/order will be immediately subject to suspension should the commentaries indicate a constitutionally adverse opinion. In the event the suspension is not sustained, the Attorney General of the United States, on behalf of The People, will pursue legal action against the offending branch. If the Court's position is sustained, the offending party will be sanctioned for violating their oath of office and endure the appropriate penalty for having done so. In the case of the congress, the sanction will be borne by the sponsors of the legislation.

A mind-numbing majority of U.S. law has absolutely no fundamental attachment to the U.S. Constitution. Most are simply an extension of errant legislative actions and having remained unopposed, these laws further metastasize as the product of abstract notions and deceptively biased interpretations all of which become the cherished Biblical-like legacy preserved and embellished by none other than practitioners of *the law* themselves.

Does one wonder how a law that requires an individual to wear a seatbelt can be passed with rapier-like efficiency yet a similar restriction barring a far more reckless act, such as violating the oath of office, will never make it past the stage of a simple query? One shouldn't wonder at all. Like all things, its resolves to a matter of choice.

The quagmire that is so nobly referred to and enforced as *the law* is merely that which influence has purchased as its preferential choice. Yes, I am angered by the elitist view that somehow ordains the legal construct as sacred and so should every American. I've observed far too many examples of abuse and hypocrisy to hold much regard for this deferential notion, particularly when the highest court of the land is populated not based on Constitutional acumen and deference but on political malleability and calculated *selective-indifference*.

There is only one body of law worthy of esteem: That which is held in deference to the emancipation of the human being as defined by one very simple yet succinct and deliberate phrase *We Hold These Truths To Be Self-Evident*! All else is calculated interpretations and aberrations aimed precisely at diluting this fundamental and providential ideal.

STIMULUS CONCEPT 6: **MILITARY**

- *Limit U.S. military actions* strictly to congressional declaration. The U.S. military is an incredibly powerful force with massive maintenance and field costs that should never be used as an extension of economic influence.

- *Mandate U.S. military command structure.* The U.S. military should never be subordinate to an international command structure of any kind. Doing so, whether by fiat or by treaty, defers the chain of command structure to non-vested authority and, more succinctly, it subrogates Constitutional authority.

- *Mandate domestic military procurement.* All U.S. military procurement must be sourced domestically if for no other reason than to preserve and enhance technological innovation, economic vitality and related security concerns. Save for select raw materials that, for geological reasons, must be sourced from outside the U.S., why would the U.S. military consider such a practice? Why would the U.S. government endorse this method of procurement? The obvious answers are not sufficient cause to support the claim that they should.

- *Constrict global deployment* of U.S. resources. As of December, 2007, the Department of Defense reports that it maintains active instillations and/or deployments in 151 countries.

The Founding Fathers specifically intended the concept of a *standing army* to be a mechanism to provide for the defense of the nation against foreign incursions and, in the case of the navy, to protect our shores and the sea-faring merchant vessels. Yes, I know there are many reasons for maintaining a global-reach military regiment; however, I see none that justify, on Constitutional grounds, a perpetual exhibition or global annexation, not to mention the associated cost to the American taxpayer for fielding such an overwhelming force.

We have all, repeatedly, heard the commentaries parroting themes such as *economic interests* or *making the world safe for democracy* however I've neither heard nor have I seen evidence that supports these positions. How has our global military establishment kept the U.S. president and congress from vaporizing our domestic economy? Or, perhaps they are referring to the foreign swarm of in-bound container ships to which this nation provides free naval escort! How has the global military presence prevented the British surrender of Hong Kong's sovereignty to China? In the case of *safe for democracy* ruse, how does one explain China, Pakistan, Afghanistan, Iran, Saudi Arabia, Lebanon, Darfur, Somalia, Argentina, Venezuela, the drug cartels in Mexico, Cuba, and so on!

"OUR GREATEST EXTENSION OF POWER WILL NOT COME AT
THE POINT OF A GUN. IT WILL COME FROM OUR ABILITY
TO PERFECT AND DEMONSTRATE THE ESTIMABLE QUALITIES
OF OUR FORM OF GOVERNMENT AND OUR ECONOMIC
PROWESS. IF SUCH IS NOT THE CASE, THEN OF COURSE I
SUSPECT WE HAVE FAR MORE SERIOUS CONCERNS."

To be sure, I am a strong supporter of the U.S. military and I agree that a component of strength must also be in military capabilities. As well, I measure incredible collateral economic benefit in the development of advanced technologies however the massive costs of maintaining a standing foreign presence is unjustified and from the vantage point of history, conspicuously treacherous in both economic and political terms. In either case, I will suggest that there are few countries on the planet unaware of the U.S. military's capabilities. Perhaps I might state the point in a slightly different form: *I'm sure they know we're here.*

A collateral point to consider: There is no winnable peace in the Middle East. Peace must no longer be a *contest* but a choice where the alternatives are not options but inspired acts of a People *drawn* to the ideals of freedom. If the U.S. approach persists, as with all nations whose history has shown a similar course and though the strategy may initially appear a success, ultimately it will mature to yield the worst possible form of defeat; the loss of life, resources, our sacred honor and a new generation of combatants.

"No nation in history has ever survived a perpetual state-of-war posture. To risk exhaustion of a nation's reserve in life and resource is the extreme expression of tyrannical rule. Our future, as a nation, will not endure or escape the costs associated with such ignorance."

It is not this or any nation's domain to replace or supplant the forces that only providence may compel. To believe that the price for this nation will differ from those who have suffered the same fate is to tempt the most rudimentary features of consequence. If there is a true and imminent threat, summarily obliterate it and by doing so curb future temptations. Barring that, we have no sound and supportable purpose for being entangled in foreign compaigns which only serve to remind us that there is no valor in pursuing an ignoble cause; we are far too long and too frequently engaged in these extended junkets. *I suggest we claim victory in preserving our national character.*

"From the volumes of history we often see only repetitions; lessons that seemingly the student is unwilling to learn."

"The tyrant, never willing to acknowledge the extremes of hubris, laughs at the diplomatic subtleties of reason. He prefers wasting his nation's resources in the campaign of folly and then having not the virtues of conscience, he seals his failures with the act of his truer form, the preference of all cowards, the capsule he saves for himself."

This is but one of the many lessons history has to offer.

STIMULUS CONCEPT 7: **ENTITLEMENT PROGRAMS**

- *Restructure Social Security.* This program typifies the evolution of the government *over promise and run* method of stewardship. This program needs to be completely overhauled; which is to say, reinvented so that it is fully and economically self-sustaining. I will discuss how this might be accomplished as a component of the section below entitled: *The Model.*

- *Restructure Medicaid and Medicare.* As with most government programs, a need that didn't exist was created to form a problem that would have otherwise never occurred. There is no economic viability in programs that have no funding mechanisms. As is the case with Social Security, Medicaid/ Medicare is a poster-child for *false-promise* government marketing and is functionally and financially unsustainable and beyond repair. The only way to address its flaws is to completely remove it from the domain of government. I will, along with Social Security, discuss how this might be accomplished as a component of the section below entitled: *The Model.*

- *Abandon the notion of government sponsored health care*[63]. I am at a loss to understand how, considering the government's track record of extreme fiscal and administrative mismanagement, any person of conscience would tempt programmed failure of this magnitude. I am fossilized with disbelief. How

---

63   Update: (3/29/10) Yes, the Health Care Reform Bill passed though I hold to the belief that if the People remain vigilant, it will never be enacted. Still, the underlying problems will remian, accordingly, these concepts are ever more relevant and exigent.

can it be that we would ever considering transferring the scope of resources required to an entity that has proven itself pathologically incapable? Fortunately, there is an approach to addressing this issue as well, and it follows in the section below entitled: *The Model.*

- *Merge or otherwise defer all government, federal and state, benefit programs to a uniform concept,* which I more fully describe in the section below entitled: *The Model.* There is no single government practice that I know of with the distinct capability of demonstrating dismissive tendencies more efficiently than in the area of public employee, included elected officials, compensation and benefits programs. Supreme elitism. Had I not spent nearly two months studying government benefits and compensation plans, I could never have imagined, nor would you, how effective government has become at manufacturing disparity. I do, however, understand why and how it is possible: *There are no economic consequences.* In any attempt to streamline the function of government with the intent of producing measurable results, the need to transform the current mess into a manageable and functional form cannot be overstated. The exception to this, for the time being, will be the medical benefits provided military personal through the Veterans Administration however certain components of military retirement benefits will have to be addressed.

- *Unfunded mandates,* as previously referenced, for Social Security and Medicare are currently $107 trillion and growing at a rate of $1.2 trillion per year and let's be clear that these amounts do not include the component costs and funding requirements for the various government (federal and state) employee retirement programs. I am very aware that these are *sacred cows* for a great many Americans who for some reason believe they are entitled to a whole-life support system funded on the backs of their fellow Americans. These government *vote-inducement programs* have got to come to an end and by doing so will, on its own, cure government deficit spending and unfunded mandate issues.

As in the private sector, every government program or entity must have a self-sustaining funding mechanism; in other words, you get the value of the benefits equal to your contribution and not one penny more. Somewhere along the way our social-culture has adopted a rather curious form which I refer to a *practical-detachment*. In its most simple form it defines *the nature and psychology of an individual or institution that awards itself emancipation from personal and social responsibility by voiding, as an incidental action, any and all relationships relevant to cause and effect.* In its most grotesque form it simply asserts: I want what I want, I don't care what it costs you, I am entitled so pay for it even if it means that someone other than the entitled goes without!

This personal quote appears in Volume I and with consideration to the current topic it would, once again, seem acutely relevant.

"WHAT ONE THINKS GOVERNMENT HAS TO GIVE
MUST FIRST UNDERSTAND IT ACCUMULATES ONLY
BY TAKING! IT OCCURS NO OTHER WAY!"

Americans are largely unaware that most government-sponsored plans are known as *defined benefit* type programs. In other words, the programs define in advance what they will pay out in benefits regardless of what the employee contributes. To some extent there have been moves, however slight, away from these *plans* through the introduction of 401(k) or thrift savings-type programs however the underlining benefits scheme is largely unchanged. Using the *defined benefit* approach in government-sponsored programs and though quite consistent with the *over-promise and run* methods, the approach is disastrous in quantitative terms. Consider the example of a government plan promising a post-retirement monthly benefit of $3,000/month[64]. Let us also assume that over a 30-year period, an individual contributed 8% of his annual salary ($36,000) to this plan for a total lifetime contribution of $86,400. To keep the illustration simple, let us assume (only) that the benefit period lasts from a retirement age of 65 and suspends at age 90 or for a projected 25 years. Over this period, the retiree would have received $900,000 in benefits in exchange for an $86,400 contribution (not considering cost of living adjustments and medical benefits)!

Ignoring administrative costs for the moment let us consider the possibility that the government managed an annual rate of return of 5% on the individual's annual contribution. At the end of 30 years the aggregate value of their contributions will be $223,281 with an unfunded mandate of $676,719 – for one retiree and not including medical benefits. Believe you me, this is a very conservative example particularly when compared to actual practices. More unbelievable are the results of similar (type) calculations when applied to actual Medicaid/ Medicare costs of care per qualified recipients when juxtaposed to the

---

64   My readership might find it interesting to note that over 6,133 retired State of California employees receive annual pensions, excluding the value of insurance benefits, of over $100,000 per year. (Source: California Public Employees Retirement System - updated as of March 2010.)

aggregate contributions made, per recipient, to these federal plans. I have made several (scenario) calculations and the ratios are beyond extreme — exceeding the unfunded mandates previously mentioned.

How could anyone receiving these benefits look at their fellow Americans and not feel a supreme sense of guilt? More so, what does it say about our culture in the case where these beneficiaries feel no shame? Furthermore, what has gone *so very wrong* with government to think it is acceptable to promise benefits that are not earned and then prescribe a system that is financially and mathematically impossible to sustain. The only possible explanation is the *selective-indifference of practical-detachment* applied to the artificial logistics of *pagan-economics*.

Before moving on to *The Model,* a few notes on health care. First, let me suggest reviewing item (11) – *Health Care Costs* – as presented in the previous chapter under the sub-heading titled *Progressive Economic Consequence.* Doing so will reacquaint one with a few examples of *why*, in this country, the health care system has deteriorated to such a near-unmanageable state. In each of the items presented in said *heading* one can clearly observe the signs of misgovernment. To that end and if for these reasons alone we should have clear cause for insisting that government be forcibly kept out of the health care industry and the health care industry kept out of government.

I do offer a *concept* that deals with the issue of health care, it is included as a collateral benefit in the following *Model.* However, as the notion of a *government sponsored health care* (GSHC) seems to be the current mantra of the day, I am compelled to make one final point on the issue before moving on to the *Model* and my point is this: Yes, if you read the polls they do suggest marginal public support for a GSHC, however, after reading the nature and scope of the questions it becomes abundantly clear that the pollster neglected to inform the respondents as to what, precisely, were the provisions of the GSHC concept being proposed. It should come as no surprise that one might anticipate an affirmative response to the following question: "Are you in favor of an insurance program that will provide you health care services, for life, at no cost?"

The GSHC concept will starve the private insurance industry, the medical research and development industry and drive medical professionals from public practice all of which will inevitably result in rationing of care. Yet another foot-print from the *over-extended and underfunded* gorilla of government excess.

"THERE IS NO REWARD OF ECONOMIC EFFICIENCIES
WHEN THERE IS NO COMPETITION AND THERE IS NO
COMPETITION WHERE THERE IS NO CHOICE!"

Setting aside for the moment the costs associated with defensive medicine and malpractice claims which GSHC does not address, the problem is not the *free-market system,* the problem is government's seemingly uncontrollable intrusions continuously redefining purpose and what becomes of common medical practices. The outcome of government's imposing itself upon the *free-market system* has grossly expanded the range of care and exposed the health care industry to massive unfunded care mandates not to mention the massive fraud and waste that accompany all government-administered programs.

The most conspicuous and measurable result of this misguided approach has been to redirect the financial burden (unfunded costs) toward the private sector the effects of which are both an explosion in costs and a degradation in quality of service. These images are but a prelude of coming attractions should GSHC become the ultimate prescription. Like many things the government does, it is beyond one's ability to comprehend and it is precisely for this reason that any attempt to reform the problem out of existence will only yield greater failure.

Lastly, for the proponents of GSHC suggesting that *rationed health care* has proven itself functional in countries such as Canada and the U.K., let me present two critical facts:

1.   Their population base is a fraction of the United States – fewer to cover. And,

2.   The standard level of health care provided is equivalent to health maintenance and acute care is severely rationed.

In support of these two points one will be pleased to know that there is an abundance of information available throughout the public domain and thus if one requires a corroborating source, little effort will be needed. Still, I think it is fair to consider the following thought:

"WHEN THE BAR OF EXPECTATION IS SET SUFFICIENTLY LOW, ONE WILL NEED TO EXPEND LITTLE EFFORT TO CLAIM SUCCESS WHEN SIMPLY FALLING OVER 'IT' IS ALL THAT IS REQUIRED!"

Before moving on, I offer an interesting bit of information which I've discovered and I must confess it has somewhat changed my outlook all together: Seems as though both Canada and the U.K. have extremely efficient pharmaceutical dispensaries[65].

---

65   Both of these countries permit the broad use of generic drugs.

THE MODEL

There are three primary components of this concept all of which revolve around one novel and guiding principle: The programs must be self-sustaining. The *three components* are as follows:

1. Establish cabinet-level position for the Benefits Standards Agency (BSA), which shall report directly to the president. This entity will be represented at the cabinet-level by a designee who is also one of this agency's five board of governors the positions thereto are arranged by congressional (the House) non-political appointments drawn only from industry-capable private-sector candidates and will consist of two, six year non-consecutive terms.

   The government will have only oversight and advisory capacities. The BSA will oversee and administrate the enterprise and shall maintain, in good order, trust investment accounts. Funds received pursuant to the functions of the BSA are confined expressly to its designated purposes and not subject to government conscription or as provided for by investment directed provisions. For purposes of investing, BSA funds shall be strictly limited to those programs described in SC-3 as government infrastructure improvements, D-C Bonds, national home mortgage fund or as described in SC-8 below. The BSA will establish and maintain a statutory expense ratio consistent with the funding and payout mandate requirements and will conform or otherwise maintain said ratio well within its operational parameters. It should be understood that the BSA will completely absorb the functions of those agencies/departments it replaces.

2. All federal and state government retirement-benefits programs will be merged into and under the jurisdiction of the BSA. The

BSA will administrate only two distinct benefits programs: The National Extended Earnings Program (NEEP)[66] and the National Health Care Program (NHCP).

3. The BSA, as part of its NHCP duties, will establish national health care coverage standards and policies aimed directly at providing a cogent format of minimum policy standards of coverage to which insurers' product lines will conform. Again, these will become minimum policy standards universally applied to all health plans and descriptions of coverage. The only exceptions to these will be the coverage/care provided by the Veterans Administration though a concerted effort should be made to merge the VA into this system.

The BSA will also establish NEEP standards which will be the universal standards applicable to all current and former federal and state government sponsored retirement benefits programs.

The two programs, conceptually, will function as follows:

NEEP:
  • Benefits will only be paid, tax free, past the attained age of 70 (eligibility age). There will be no state mandated retirement age. In other words, you retire when you can afford too.

  • Benefits will be paid, upon means-tests authentication, on combined earned and/or unearned household annual incomes of under $150,000, inclusive of all retirement benefits and/or direct/indirect income sources. Those household incomes over $150,000 will be limited to actual contribu-

---

66   NEEP — though not intended, I find this acronym a great source of laughter. Perhaps we may need to develop a different acronym, something a bit more banal.

tions made. Payment duration options shall range from 2-15 year terms.

- Benefits paid to eligible recipients whose date of birth (DOB) is before 1955 will receive payment consistent with direct Social Security systems payment benefits no less than those currently provided as of 2010. The federal[67] and state[68] governments will directly fund the BSA-NEEP trust fund in an amount equal to those specified benefits requirements by instructing the Federal Reserve to electronically transfer funds directly into a trust account designated exclusively for these recipients.

- Benefits paid to eligible recipients whose DOB is 1956 or thereafter will receive benefits based solely on direct contributions (DC) made by said recipient. DC's will accrue at a minimum statutory rate of 4.5%.

- Job related disability benefits will be equal to those paid at eligibility age, had the cumulative annual average contribution, pre-disability, been continued. For benefits claims made for non-job related disabilities, benefits will be limited to direct contributions made. The NHCP (below) will offer supplemental disability benefit options.

---

67   Federal government contributions will be to the extent of: (1) Pre-1955 recipients: an amount equal to meet 2010 cutoff funding requirements to a live expectancy age of 85. And (2) Post-1956 recipients: an amount equal to actual participant contributions made.

68   State government contributions will be to the extent of: (1) Retiree benefits: an amount equal to but not less than actual contributions made or an amount sufficient to generate a rate no less than 48% of their current retirement benefit. And (2) Active employees: to the extent of actual participants contributions made.

- Direct-contributions (DCs) shall be mandatory for all U.S. citizens at a minimum rate of 5% of their *annual household gross income exemption* (AHGIE). As part of the NEEP and NHCP there will be no federal or state income tax or assessment of any kind levied on the first $350,000 of combined household incomes (the AHGIE). To accommodate the need or desire for an increased retirement benefit, there will be no limits on DC's.

- BSA-NEEP will establish an online resource for individuals to retrieve information on their benefits accruals and a calculator to provide illustrations for future benefits based on additional direct-contributions.

- Except for as provided for herein, there will be no benefits paid beyond those accrued by or through direct contributions.

- There will be no restrictions on private retirement plans; however, it is important to note the BSA-NEEP program benefits have direct offset provisions. Under these circumstance, DC's made shall be returned in similar form to those for household incomes, post age 70, in excess of $150,000.

NHCP:

Like the NEEP system, the National Health Care Program is intended to conform and function in the manner described in the *three-components* provided above. This *concept*, NHCP, is intended to operate as an oversight and developmental advisory possessing authority with influence similar to that of a public utility commission (PUC) or an Industry Standards Board.

The following are operational and functional guidelines for the program:

- Establish public, medical and insurance industry consensus as to minimum policy standards of coverage consistent with minimum medical standards of practice. It will be NHCP policy that these be uniform industry-wide standards. Specific attention should be directed to addressing ER, ICU, psychiatric, alternative medicine, experimental medicine, generic drug development and end-of-life procedure care limits. Uniform claims procedures should also be developed accommodating minimum standards of efficiency.

- Consideration should be given to establishing a menu offering different types of coverage and due to the nature and scope of age-specific care requirements, consideration should be given to *pre* and *post* age 70 *pools*. Examples of *menu-coverage* are as follows: (1) Minimum major medical coverage. (2.) Extended-expanded care coverage. (3.) *Dollar-one* medical coverage. (4.) ER coverage rider. (5.) Health maintenance coverage rider. (6.) Disability/unemployment income riders. (7.) Maternity coverage rider. (8.) Dental coverage rider. (9.) Long-term care rider. (10.) Foreign travel coverage and so on. Premiums should be established as *individual* or as *family* with separate premium factors for family size and, as well, a *no-age-based* premium structure within the two distinct pools.

- The insurance industry should be encouraged to create broad risk pools to insure diversity of risk and to monetize above average costs associated with disproportionate and coincidental risk factors associated with a company's client base. Additionally, an absorption protocol, in the event of a competitor's dissolution, should be developed.

- All insurance companies, regardless of industry specialty, should be encouraged to diversify their scope of coverage to include providing health insurance pursuant to the provisions developed herein; the broader the risk pool, the more efficiently managed the system risks and expenses. There should be strictly defined prohibitions as to the nature and type of investments in which companies are permitted to participate. Insurance companies participating in the NHCP program will benefit from a 3% taxable income rate-exemption (health insurance divisions only) for those who operate at or below the grading agency's expense load factor average.

- Upon establishing developmental consensus, the insurance industry will develop individual offerings (noting minimum policy standards) and associate premiums which shall be reviewed by BSA-NHCP administrators and issues addressed accordingly.

- An appropriate grading agency should be engaged to establish rigid and verifiable information as to operational and functional practices of each participating company. Example: investment pool risk grade, liquidity grade, expense-load factor, etc.

- Upon perfecting the various program offerings and related premiums, the programs will be mass marketed directly to the public with a one-time, no pre-existing conditions limitation as well as a provision that guarantees coverage once enrolled so long as participation breaks do not exceed a lifetime aggregate of 12 months. It should be made clear in all marketing material that these programs, although not mandatory, replace all government sponsored (including state) health insurance programs and that absent participation "you break, you pay."

- NHCP costs/premiums will be paid directly as withholdings from an individual's payroll check. Self-employed will pay their premiums directly through auto-bank draws or credit/debit card drafts.

- As in the case with NEEP, upon providing appropriate documentation authenticating annual premium payments, there will be no federal or state income tax of any kind levied on the first $350,000 of combined household income.

- All programs will be completely transportable.

- Upon establishing the premium structure for *minimum major medical coverage* in the *+70 pool*, the BSA-NHCP will establish funding requirements for current *+70* current (as of 2009) participants in the existing Medicaid/Medicare programs. For those participants receiving benefits due to long-term disabilities, the BSA-NHCP will establish funding requirements to insure continued coverage. Once these combined costs are determined, the Federal Reserve Bank will electronically transfer funds directly into BSA trust accounts whose specific purposes are to accrue and dispense premiums for these pools as they come due. The program does not provide for unfunded prescription drug benefits; however, the program will provide rider option.

- Consideration should also be given to establishing an optional self-insured risk pool or a specific form of coverage applicable to health care providers. The purpose of this is to provide a universal funding mechanism for indigent care; however, strict limits on *level of care* should be established with expanded care coverage options available to avoid the risk of this feature becoming an "escape-valve" for those who should otherwise be enrolled in the primary care plans previously mentioned.

- Protocols should be developed to capture individuals receiving public benefits of any kind and a fee structure should be levied on these to enjoin those who are consumers of care with, at the minimum, a component responsibility for the cost of providing the same. Similar in the case, as an example, are states who mandate minimum automobile coverage and tie its enforcement to auto licensing.

These programs are designed to discourage *whole life support system* mentality. They are truly functional and noble in their purpose while maintaining direct, free market influences. In the case of the NHCP, the programs offer basic coverage as well as leaving open the opportunity for insurance companies to further *option-equip* basic coverage with extended benefits such as maternity and dental, to name only two.

The only items, though I am sure there may be others, that are conspicuously left out of these programs are inmate care, long-term indigent and psychiatric care. These issues will need to be left to the respective states to consult with the BSA and establish functional protocols, coverage and funding mechanisms. The life choices of an individual are not our national burden and likewise should never be treated as such.

These two programs have significant collateral benefits the most obvious of which is resolving the unmanageable administrative and funding costs to both the federal and state governments (the U.S. taxpayer) and removing both from a function far beyond their functional and practical domain. These programs place the financial and administrative burden precisely where it should be and that is in the hands of those individual receiving benefits and those who provide them. It encourages the beneficial effects of *tortional-economic*-tension – a cost management mechanism discussed in Volume II of this series – promoting administrative efficiencies and economic incentive as a reward.

There is a significant problem with this concept and I owe you, the reader, an honest admission. The federal government and the *pagan-economists* will strongly object to these programs for two very simple reasons:

1. These programs remove the government from the financial control and administrative process. And,

2. Few Americans are aware that the money collected for Social Security and Medicaid/Medicare, through payroll taxes, actually never makes it into these funds. By excising the government from its role as a tax-collector, government also must surrender the influence this financial control purchases. They will not go quietly and despite the soundness of these proposals, they will, nonetheless, strenuously and creatively object to them.

In the end, something will need to be done as the government's impulse-driven spending practices have collapsed the system. The only possible alternatives are to increase taxes and cut benefits. If you look closely, very closely at the recently passed (March, 2010) Health Care Reform bill, that's precisely what they've done.

STIMULUS CONCEPT 8: **ECONOMIC**

- *Suspend individual income tax.* For a period of three years, completely suspend individual income tax and the collateral applications of the *alternative minimum tax* for net taxable, *non-passive*, household incomes under $350,000[69]. This will promote consumer spending and provide the opportunity for alternative *test* revenue-generating concepts to be developed. The ultimate goal is to get out of the direct income tax model which is a testament to government's dysfunctional approach to revenue generation and into some form of means or point of purchase tax for individuals only.

- The objections will, of course, be from those who suggest that the government can ill-afford the loss in tax revenues; my response of course is that if something isn't done soon, there will be no income sufficient to tax. As it stands, household gross incomes are plummeting so I see little cause for concern as to tax revenues. I find it equally interesting that the government concern for loss of revenues shows little or

---

69   This concept would be integrated with the provisions of The Model as discussed above. I recommend, as well, suspending tax credits of all types all of which are simply scurrilous re-apportionments which contribute to the ineffectiveness of the Internal Revenue Code.

no deference to the shrinking revenue generating capacity of the individual.

- *Raise (double) the U.S. corporate tax rate* and eliminate foreign income tax offsets against domestic tax liability. Yes, you heard it right! Since 1950, the individual taxpayer burden has consistently averaged just over 8% of GDP[70] or 45% of government revenues.[71] Whereas for the same period corporate tax revenues have fallen from "…between 5 and 6 percent of GDP in the early 1950s to 2.1 percent of GDP in 2008"[72] or less than 12% of the government's revenues.[73] By appropriately redirecting and restructuring the tax burden we move toward a functional wealth-creating economy. Here are a few additional *points* on the subject:

1. Permit dividend distributions (common stock only and within limits) as offsets against taxable income. This would promote investment in corporate securities (new issues) and as the income to investors would be passive, the tax burden would be at the individual level.

2. Increasing the tax burden at the corporate level would encourage focused business development by redirecting excess capital liquidity to be applied to further research and development, which, in-turn, expand business productivity and efficiencies.

---

70   Urban Institute and Brookings Institution – Tax Policy Center, "Tax Topic" March, 2009

71   ibid

72   ibid

73   ibid

3. Compatible with this approach is the concepts discussed in *The Model* whereby business is no longer burdened by benefits costs, cash flow is now improved to enhance employee compensations as well.

4. Eliminating the tax bias inherent in the present system also tends to eliminate the bias of questionable corporate influence and government bias. I would encourage my readership to review the discussion in Volume II: *Value Given, Value Received* in the section titled "Confirmation of Excess," which begins on page 48.

The goal here is to restructure the tax system to encourage a wealth-creating economy and to create a sustainable economic cycle built on a concept I refer to as *progenerative economics*[74]. Corporations, in effect, have a tax-haven status under the current system due to various accounting and special treatment features. The net affect of this is an extremely biased and unjustified economic advantage depriving the government of a more appropriate, as intended, revenue generating source. Tax revenues, at the individual level, must be assessed only on passive income and excess active net-incomes and never on the wealth generated on the labors of the individual. Never! At the individual level, this is nothing but what it is: enslavement! Enterprises and individuals should, through a pro-generative

---

74   Progenerative Economics: An economic philosophy best characterized by the term: "intuitive-adaptability," which is the complete antithesis of conventional (theoretical) business cycles: incubation-expansion-exhaustion. The model postulates that the "exhaustion" phase, also thought of as recession/depression cycle, can be eliminated by interdigitating the expansion-incubation phase and thereby perpetuating a more progenerative economic cycle. The theory intimates that economic degeneration occurs from either or both concepts defined as: (a.) convenient-fatigue and/or (b.) predatory-acquisition.

tax system, be encouraged to exceed peak performance and never, as presently designed, to escape it. Every possible effort should be expended to eliminate, at every level of government, parasitic taxes that feed off wealth-creating cycles.

- *Immediately enforce a lost opportunity tax (LOT)* of 15% (based on *retail values*) on all imported finished goods and states should agree to limit their respective sales taxes structures to no more than 3.5%; if they do not, The People of each state should, by state constitutional amendment, insist that the value added/excise taxes be restricted. There is no such thing as economic interests outside the borders of these United States. If you should hear any politician, economist, corporate spokesperson, etc. suggesting otherwise, you have my permission to tar and feather them.

If, as it appears likely, you should hear someone commenting on trade policies (treaties) as protectionist in nature, do not argue with him, understand that it is likely this individual has no idea what he or she is talking about. *Protectionism* is one of those convenient user-selective applications; they are always used by an individual wanting to assert an unsupportable claim in such a way as to negate one's native or unalienable principles which, when engaged by an alert individual, can easily defeat their claim.

"GOVERNMENT ALWAYS DEFERS TO WHAT BECOMES
A PREFERENTIAL AMBITION, ONLY TO CAMOUFLAGE
A FAULT THEY'D RATHER NOT ADDRESS."

I believe there is sufficient support for my comment if only one considers this country's political and economic crisis. Counsel these folks to read SC-4 above. Wealth creating industries need to be returned to the United States.

- *Establish a corporate income tax surcharge* on income generated on products or services sourced from outside the United States. This may not be quite obvious and though I mentioned the issue of *transfer pricing* in an earlier volume[75], corporations have extraordinarily creative accounting techniques for depressing taxable revenues by increasing inventory costs of foreign-sourced product. Additionally, the epidemic of outsourcing not only has to stop, the domestic *wealth-creating* function must be restored. This issue needs to be addressed and the most effective way is via *punitive tax* burden. This type of tax burden, when used in this manner, is precisely the type of *revenue generating feature* I speak of when, in Volume II: *Value Given, Value Received* under the title of "Simple Economics", I refer to the government generating tax revenues as an "advocate of the economic system."

- *Promote the establishment of designated corporate opportunity bonds.* This would be a new form of bond created to promote investment in domestic wealth creating enterprises. The returns on these bonds would be tax free to the extent the underlying corporate revenues are generated from domestically-sourced product/output. The BSA trusts, referenced in

---

75   A wonderful discussion on the subject of transfer-pricing occurs in Volume I: We Hold These Truths in the section titled "Free Trade vs. Protectionism," which begins on page 55 therein.

The Model (following SC-7), would be permitted to invest in these types of bonds.

- *Encourage corporate reinvention and adaptation of emerging technological research and product development.* Why has corporate America abandoned domestic research and development of adaptation/replacement of emerging technologies? Why have companies such as General Electric not pursued domestic development and production for applications in the most basic of applications? Example(s): The replacement of incandescent light-bulbs with *light emitting diode* (L.E.D.), advanced induction-motor technologies, advanced manufacturing technologies (robotics) and this list is near endless.

- I truly hope the day is fast approaching when the notion of a sustainable service-based economy, global economic micro-management as well as global warming are seen for the extreme eccentricities that they have show themselves to be.

- *Encourage restoration of base industries* and the development of an integrated, cross-purpose and extremely adaptable industrial model. The mantra should be: *If it is consumed here, it should be produced here.* In the few areas where products and services cannot be sourced domestically, these may be considered, under certain circumstances, *tariff-exempt.*

- *Encourage individual states to become more economically independent.* Self-sustaining economic models should be promoted at the state and local levels and every effort to void the temptations toward *mass-retail*[76] concepts should be engaged. The only way to create economic sustainability – adaptability and ultimately durability – is to model and/or create strong independent economic regimens. By enforcing this concept at the state and local level, the concept aids in blocking the global fracturing of a national economy. One has only to observe the rotting effects of *mass-retail* on inner-city structures to endorse this posit.

• *Establish precise product origin labeling.* Concealing the origins of a product is nothing short of fraud. Consider the health risks this country has been exposed to by foreign-sourced food products, which, under current labeling prac-tice the consumer is unable to affect even the most basic self-preservation functions. There is a serious problem with an environment that nurtures a government policy that would willingly expose a people to this type of risk. There is no sound explanation for this — none!

• *Transference of advanced technologies.* As mentioned in the SC-6 above, the U.S. military, including N.A.S.A., must be prohibited from sourcing all product, material and services from outside the United States industrial base. This includes the United States government as well. However, placing this aside, the government technology complex is an incred-

---

76   Mass-Retail is a euphemism applied to the expansion of economic blight typically observed by the large retail-centers and box stores usually endorsed by municipalities in search of greater sales-tax revenues. They are largely the product of coercive-planning by city managers who impose theoreti-cal community planning concepts resulting in incongruent urban-sprawl, lost opportunity, expanded infrastructure demands and maintenance costs not supported by the increased revenue generation. Most often they result in displacement of economic independence and maturation.

ible source for technology transfer to the domestic/private economy. Which leads to the following Concept:

- *Establish proprietary rights to advance technologies* developed under government contract. What a fabulous way for the government to generate revenues, and by the way, the idea is congruent with constitutional provisions. If taxpayer funds are used to develop a resource or technology that migrates into an economic cycle, the taxpayer/government should be receiving monetary rewards, e.g., royalties, etc., from these technologies.

- *Don't go green, just go away!* The issue of global warming and the flighty nauseous notions of green technologies have incredibly dangerous economic, industrial and national consequences that also trend toward an inherent fault that I will simply refer to as a *national economic bias* (explained below). In a fully functioning economy, the likes of which we've promoted throughout this *Series,* simple standards and punitive judicial measures would be all that is required to address reckless and dangerous environmental practices.

I realize that the sight of acres-upon-acres of wind farms will send the eco-conscious into an apoplectic state of nirvana, if that's even possible; however, the realities are that to replace the productive capacity of a coal-fired power generator would require unjustified capital investment in procurement and maintenance. And frankly, wind farms are a complete eye-sewer! Fact of the matter is this: The technology presently exists to make all fossil-fuel combustive processes near emission-neutral. Our nation is better served by pursuing disciplined net-positive technological advancement and not the apocryphal notion of impulse-driven fantasy.

The *national economic bias* occurs in two specific instances: (1.) Global environmental treaties inherently penalize the developed nations. For any discriminating mind it should be quite obvious that the U.S. consumes more energy than most nations and for two very simple reasons: (a) there are approximately 300 million Americans, and perhaps less obvious, (b) I suspect there are very few mud-huts in the Andes Mountains that have the electrical demands equal to that of a typical American or Western European home. A point few seem to consider. (2) Unless the eco-tech is developed, manufactured and installed by domestic U.S. resources then there is treble damages to the U.S. economy in each of these specific economic components: Technology, industry and labor. Case in point: Of the $2.2 billion in alternative energy grants sanctioned thus far from funds made available via the 2009 stimulus bill, only $500 million went to U.S. firms[77].

Until we detach ourselves from the adolescent "eco-green" euphoria, the pursuit of sound ecological and environmental management will only be conversation for wheat-grass parties. Which leads to the next:

- *Develop and redevelop infrastructure improvements* based on sound environmental policy. There is incredible economic

---

77   American University report: Blown Away date 2/8/10 citing U.S. Department of Energy references which dispute the accuracies of the AU Report though DOE was unable to specify the items in dispute. Regardless, even if the AU Report is off by 50% I trust the point is made, none-the-less, sufficiently relevant.

opportunity in developing technologies for rerouting overhead power lines into underground conduits. Incredible tree-saving opportunities exist in developing composite (including metal) framing materials. In the residential housing segment of the economy alone, the opportunities for economic reinvention are near infinite!

- I'm of the opinion that Mother Earth is completely detached from our reality: In other words, even if we were to take all four-five billion of us humans and somehow manage, even if for only one day, to fit all of us side by side on the island of Cuba I seriously doubt we will alter the rotation of the earth about its axis and try as we might, we are not going to keep the volcanoes from erupting! Yes, Mother Earth has her affairs in order and despite the absence of evidence to the contrary, she is conspicuously doing quite well! However, personally, I suspect she'd favor our suspending use of the increadibly toxic nickel metal hydride batteries which are used in hybrid vehicles.

- *Government-sponsored national rail system.* This is one of the few government projects that has the possibility of being a wealth creating enterprise if developed using a non-government approach. The system should be designed in such a way as to use existing right of ways, possibly elevated, providing service in a cross-corridor (national grid) manner. The domestic development and manufacturing should be focused in such a way as to make the system modular and its infrastructure uniform to both national, regional and local systems insuring both adaptability, economic efficiencies and ultimately by every means possible, economically self-sustaining.

Funding will be made available through the combined uses of the D-C Bonds referenced in SC-3 above and as well, this is the type of *self-revenue generating* project eligible for BSA Trust Investment as referenced in *The Model* previously discussed. It should be a GSE autonomous-type entity with oversight (only) by the U.S. Treasury and Department of Transportation.

Amtrak's failure is not of conceptual origins, it is merely a pro-totypical dysfunction that is the nature of all government-run entities — the U.S. Postal Service suffers for much the same reason. These organizations are doomed to economic failure largely because their mandates are not driven by economic efficiencies. They are, functionally, designed to fail. Each of these, in truth, was among the candidates that contributed to my development of the concepts of *Systemic Cost Multiplier Effect* and *Physio-Sociological Economics* (PSE)[78].

They, of course, can be made to work however their models will have to be adapted to functional and sustainable realities. What is interesting to note is that each of these examples possesses a uniquely native and organic demand that by its nature commands the ideal economic opportunity: *A demand in search of supply.* In the case of Amtrak, the demand for transport (humans), in the case of the Postal

78   See footnotes #30 and #31 as they appear in Volume II: Value Given, Value Received and the related discussion to which each of these are attached.

Service, the very same demand for transport (mail). There's no excuse for these failures.

- *Reverse, suspend or otherwise vaporize all government bailout and stimulus plans* before further damage is done. These programs represent "drunken sailor" political-mentality at its absolute worst: detached as to form and dysfunctional as to practice. The federal government, at the time of this writing, has accomplished near-total departure from positive-planned outcome. They have used taxpayer funds to subsidize *union ownership* of a publicly held company (GM and Chrysler). Of equal interest to you should be yet another federal government subsidy relating to the purchase of a U.S. automobile company (Chrysler), rather circuitously, by its previous owner (Daimler) who just happens to possess an equity position[79] in the new co-owner (Fiat, SpA.) whose, just to be sure the point is not lost, purchase was also subsidized by the U.S. government. Put the money to a productive and meaningful use for a change. Try the following on for size:

- *Write down all owner-occupied mortgages.* The bubble is still bursting and as of this writing, the effects of the commercial real estate collapse, which will severely destabilize the invested reserves of insurance companies and institutional investors and further fracture the banking system, are only just beginning to surface.

---

79   It is important to note that in March of 2009 I had confirmed the Daimler ownership of Fiat, Spa directly from the corporate website. By July of 2009, while the government was proceeding through finalizing the U.S. Government sponsored transaction, I happened to visit the website once again and discovered that the Investor Relations tab that contained major stockholders information had been removed.

Instead of saving what has already been lost, the so-called toxic assets, why not protect what has been earned but is at risk due to circumstance out of a property owner's control? There is absolutely *no reason* to not consider a *write-down* of owner-occupied mortgages as it represents but a fraction of what the Federal Reserve has quietly sent to foreign central banks and/or what the government has wasted in bailouts, dysfunctional stimulus packages and the Troubled Asset Relief Program (TARP). Straight across the board 30% "write down" of all mortgages balances for all owner-occupied residence with no prejudice of any kind.

• *Reinvent public education system.* There's much to write on this subject though suffice to say, we need a national commitment to quality education and not a political discussion or one the revolves around territorial disputes or despotic tendencies. There is no soundness to a solution whose first commitment is to heave billions of dollars at a problem whose existence is not a function of funding but rather one of form and purpose-filled function. Further, although the standards are and should be national in scope, in order for the process to be responsive and possess a tactile sense of urgency and efficiency, the process must be administered at the local level.

Most states are vulnerable to internal and external political biases consuming far too much of the available resources. In the end, the children and the nation's social and economic health suffers. For this reason, consideration should be given to developing an autonomous GSE-type model similar to that mentioned in SC 7 and although funding is received from the federal/state governments the administrative process must be protected from political and external influences.

"WHEN THE DOMAIN OF GOVERNMENT EXPANDS BEYOND ITS BOUNDARIES AND INTO THE MURKY WATERS OF SELF-DEALING, BE ASSURED THAT BOTH PURPOSE AND INTENTION BECOME WHATEVER THEY CHOOSE TO BE."

Teachers must also be able to *opt-out* of the unions in favor of alternative mediation methods integrated into the GSE-like entity as mentioned above. The inherent bias that is the systemic nature of all union (type) organizational structures should be sufficient reason to prohibit access, of any kind, to the table of discourse responsible for administrating so precious and critical a function. National education standards must include mandatory English-only curricula, including, at the minimum, American history and constitutional government, sciences, math, logic and classical studies, at age appropriate levels, for every year from K through 12. I also believe there should be enforced standards of decorum and dress; the outward actions and appearances of an individual directly mirror his or her internal covenant. *Character is cultured, not coincidental.*

The education system must be restored to a form that is designed to instill estimable qualities that will mature along with a lifetime of learning and individual productivity. A child must know of his or her nation's heritage and systems, how to function and how to think! If, after the ninth grade, a student is unwilling to meet the minimum educational standards, consideration should be given to establishing a military-type preparatory school with emphasis on *trade schooling* and/or *military service*.

As I am firmly committed to the unalienable right of self-determination, this ideal applies equally to education. Accordingly, choice is critical and an absolute necessity for the parent whose ambition to have the best possible education for their child must be met with an education system capable of delivering. If we prefer that no child fall through the cracks, then I would suggest that we begin with sealing each void. To that end, a *voucher system* is an absolute must as mediocrity should never be the choice offered or imposed upon a parent or their child and if a voucher-system offers the means to apply *tortional-economic-tensions[80]* to the business of education, then by all means this economic force must be efficiently enabled.

At the university level I dare say the notion of *Value Given, Value Received* is, in much the same way as the public school system is a completely foreign concept, particularly when one considers the irreconcilable costs. As a way-station for perpetual spring break-like intellectual plagiarism, the system is a stunning success. True, there are a few institutions that deliver an extraordinary academic board of fare; however, it is more likely that the National Football and Basketball Leagues, on economic terms, are the two greatest benefactors of the U.S. college and university system. *Delivering the least possible*

---

80   "Tortional economic tension": A term from Volume II: Value Given, Value Received that describes the organic/"native" forces applied to or confronted by an economic function serving to expose and eliminate deficiencies as a means to compel the refinement toward positive measured outcome. This is, in effect, the self-perfecting component of the "native economy."

value for the highest possible price is a rather dubious ambition: The outcome is an under-qualified debt-laden graduate. From my point of view, this is not a survivable measure of achievement.

I may be in the company of one on this last point; however, I truly do believe that the value of education is not so much teaching or the memorization of information but more so the cultivating of an intuitive and adaptable thought process whereby an individual is equipped to think and project the same processes, applicably, in or to a dynamic environment so as to expose that which is not known. *Adaptable, intuitive and self-reliant may very well be concepts upon which we might shape both a functionally productive and vibrant educational as well as economic system.*

To be sure, there are many more areas of opportunity to explore and in the few (above) I have identified, there is more to be done in attenuating each. Nonetheless, as a genesis for what may come of our world, I've endeavored to target those areas that are the most conspicuous and most critical. In more ways than one, there truly are no limits.

What is remarkably exciting to me is that all of these can be effected quite easily. What is required is a common mind that is willing to see their value and a penetrating sense of purpose and urgency to bring them to life. To be completely blunt, we need to restore a sense of unifying purpose across the American landscapes and this starts with Stimulus Concept #1 – *Reconstitution* and proceeds from there.

"ECONOMIC VITALITY CAN BE INSPIRED FROM ABOVE, BUT IT WILL ALWAYS AND ONLY EVER PROPAGATE FROM THE BOTTOM UP!"

What is required from each of us is a combination of both revolution-ary and evolutionary posture — and clearly these are concepts quite foreign to the bureaucracies of government. Our current government is not unlike a beached whale dying in the midday sun, not knowing how it got there and no longer caring that it has. I have, on a daily basis, deliberately and persistently combed the media outlets for any signs of cogent and specific strategy for a national recovery; even a token gesture would have captured my attention, but there are none to be had. It appears that this nation is finally coming around to the truth that government has grown so far beyond reasonable and practicable limits for this nation to be able to survive the continuous occurrence of strategic and systemic failure at any level of government.

Yes, of course, there is an abundance, on a daily basis, of hackneyed ref-erences to reclaiming past successes or the nebulous ramblings of past administrations' renditions yet I have seen no specifics, nothing regen-erative and certainly nothing that fuels creative discourse or presents a declaration around which we, as a nation, might assemble. No, only the regurgitations of past failures and political nostrums.

My contribution is a sincere attempt aimed at overcoming the mental gridlock and the political malaise; this entire *Series* is a monument to this single ambition. Whatever one may think of these concepts, the fact remains; we do have choices!

There is grand success ahead; however, as in all things worth accom-plishing, it will require a bold approach, one that rejects the failed political and economic practices of drudgery, deception and the bias of undo influence and progressive folklore. It will require the application of fundamental principles each focused upon one single solitary moti-vation and that is social, political and economic revitalization!

No nation functions in decline, it only further succumbs to the weight of flawed policies. These are not suppositions or hyperbole, these are facts supported by the course of history and if you think crisis loves a vacuum, well listen up: I hear "Hoovers!" It is vital, once again, to consider this: There is no middle ground in the practiced art of resuscitation; there is only success or surrender!

> "HE HAS WON THE BATTLE WITH HIMSELF, AND
> THAT ACCORDING TO WHAT HE'S TOLD ME, IS THE
> GREATEST VICTORY ANYONE COULD WANT."[81]

81   "Don Quixote" by Don Miguel de Cervantes

Closing Comments

"I've no need for vision to see what I know to be true."

WHATEVER MIGHT BE SAID or thought or written as to the totality of this effort, one comment I would treasure most would be to hear it said, "He loves all things American!" I love the land and I love our People. Most of all, I love the ideals that define what is the very essence of American. It is no longer only a continent or nation, it is, in fact, its own *ideal*. I have also discovered that I am not alone in these sentiments and because of this;

I am not prepared to *Stand4* the world as it is, I am not prepared to *Stand4* a belief system that would squander my providential rights and I am not prepared to *Stand4* a system that will scar the landscape that my or your children will have to endure. NO, *I Stand4* a world full of promise, I *Stand4* a world whose vision is shared by those who also revere Providential Design! Yes indeed, I *Stand4* those truths that we hold in common as self-evident: *Life, Liberty and the Pursuit of Happiness*! Will you *Stand4* each of these along with me and countless others?

Your response, of course, is demonstrated by action — the first indication of which was in evidence the moment you opened the first page of Volume I: *We Hold These Truths*.

"A WILLING HEART IS REQUIRED TO EXPRESS OUT LOUD
WHAT IS OTHERWISE CONCEALED IN SILENT DESPERATION.
WHEN TAKING (IF ONLY ONE) A STEP TOWARD THAT WHICH
ONE DESIRES, THAT WHICH IS THE OBJECT OF YOUR
INTENTION TAKES ONE STEP EVER CLOSER TO YOU."

I was once asked that if I were able to travel back in time, what person would I most want to meet. This acquaintance was surprised by my answer as she thought I'd say Jesus or Thomas Jefferson. I responded, saying, "No, meeting Jesus would be far too difficult as I would sense he'd know my failures and I would be devastated should he think his efforts had been wasted on me. Thomas Jefferson, on the other hand, would likely only find me amusing and a bit long winded!" Yes, I would love to have met and sat with him for a spell, one that I'd hope might last for months. I'd want to witness, first hand, if all that has been written about him was possible to be confined to one man. This comment would be appropriate to both men.

There are many historically significant people and events that mark history's log and reciting each would be a novel unto itself; however, there is another individual who stirs both my admiration and curiosity. I've been to his home, *The Hermitage,* and I have read much about his life. Yet there is a particular period in his life that would be of specific interest to me: The weeks before the Battle of New Orleans and then the moment following his final victory over the British. The contrast in both of his perspectives would have been fascinating as this victory, arguably, confirmed to the world powers of the day that the United States of America was, finally, to be *a nation among nations.* I'm sure he must have known, or at least sensed, a measured degree of inevitability. I draw the previous observation from his own words:

*"Americans are not a perfect people, but
we are called to a perfect mission."*

From events and thoughts such as this, please do ponder my final
offering;

"WE, AS A PEOPLE, FIND OURSELVES AS THE LATEST GENERATION,
POSSESSORS OF THE HERITAGE OF FREEDOMS WON BY THOSE
WHO HAVE COME BEFORE AND BY THOSE WHO SILENTLY WALK
AMONG US. AS WE MUST LOOK TO THE DECADES PAST AND
EVEN UNTO THIS DAY, WE MUST ASK OURSELVES TO ACCOUNT
FOR THAT WHICH WE HAVE TAKEN FROM THOSE WHO HAVE
GIVEN SO MUCH. HAVE WE BORNE THE YOKE OF DUTIES OWED
TO SACRED FIRES AND BLOOD-SOAKED LANDS AND FORGOTTEN
FIELDS? DOES ONE'S HEART STIR AT THE IMAGED FIST AS SHE
BEARS OUR SACRED FLAME AND WHOSE VOICE IS BUT A WHISPER
IN LANDS WHO HAVE YET TO CLAIM THESE AS THEIR OWN?

I LOOK AT FACES STERN AND SOUR WHO CLAIM THIS CAUSE
YET STAND FOR NONE. ONE MUST CONSIDER; WOULD THEY
SURRENDER POSTURING AND STAND FOR NONE THEY KNOW?

WE KNOW OF FREEDOM, YET IGNORE ITS COST, SQUANDERING ITS
VALUE, ONCE PRICELESS, NOW SEEMINGLY LOST. GOD HIMSELF
MUST WONDER IF HE ERRED UPON A COMMON BOND WE BRUSH
SO THOUGHTLESSLY ASIDE ONLY THEN TO VAINLY BLUSH.

WE MUST KNOW THERE IS SUCH SADNESS IN THOSE
WHOSE HOPE UPON THIS NATION WAS HELD IN SOVEREIGN
TRUST. A ONCE FIERCE AND STURDY STRUCTURE WHOSE
SOLEMN VOW WAS PROUD, FORTHRIGHT AND JUST.

KNOWING SACRED NOT AS PASSING FANCY BUT AS AN ETERNAL
AND LASTING SCRIPT; THIS NATION WAS INSPIRED BY A QUEST,
A NOBLE AND LASTING CAUSE WHOSE FOUNDATIONS SPEAK OF
IDEALS INSCRIBED IN BRILLIANT TERMS CONVEYED BY MIND
OF PROVIDENTIAL FORM. IT IS NOT A QUESTION ON WHICH TO
QUERY BUT ONE WHICH SPEAKS IN FINITE TERMS AND NOT OF
COINCIDENTAL OPTION OR PARODY OF CHOICE. NO, THE FAVOR
WE REQUIRE LIES WITHIN THE EASE OF ABSOLUTES; AWAITS
THE PATIENT CHAMBERS OF A STILL AND TIMELESS VOICE.

YOU WHO HOLD THE SACRED FLAME ARE CALLED OUT AND CALLED
UPON TO STAND AND BEAR AS YOUR OWN AND WITNESS THAT
WHICH YOU ALONE PRESERVE - SO STAND AND BE STEADY AS YOU
RAISE YOUR FLAME. STAND AND BE STEADY! STAND AND BE HEARD!"

To appreciate these words as I intend is also to understand the meaning
of the title of this last Volume of the *Series: Valor in Prosperity*. There is
strength of mind and spirit such that when *in* the face of overwhelming obstacles, it silently appears in the heart of a person who grasps the
timelessness of necessity and somehow finds the willingness to endure
the burden and yet never once considers the cost or sacrifice.

"THE SELFLESSNESS IS PALPABLE, THE RIGORS UNTHINKABLE AND THE OUTCOME UNIMAGINABLY TRANSFORMATIVE: THIS IS VALOR IN PROSPERITY, THE UNKNOWN REWARDS THAT EMERGE WHEN ONE IGNORES THE PRICE, THE SACRIFICE AND THE OBSTACLES!"

It is for this and perhaps a few other reasons that I would dearly love to have interviewed Andrew Jackson before and after the Battle of New Orleans.

To close, please do know that I have enjoyed, immensely, applying the effort necessary to prepare this material for your thoughtful consideration and study. You have, by now, indulged my peculiar writing style and my tendency to wax a bit long winded. For this and for many reasons, I am most grateful and will eagerly look for your faces along the roads I've yet to travel.

For whatever may become of the ideals sheltered by this beloved land and our American family the world over, in the years and centuries that follow, for all time in this – the *Blind Vision Series* – my most treasured effort, I will have recorded my thoughts and my greatest hopes for our best years yet to come!

"I WOULD RATHER BE EXPOSED TO THE INCONVENIENCES ATTENDING TOO MUCH LIBERTY THAN TO THOSE ATTENDING TOO SMALL A DEGREE OF IT."[82]

Not an *End*, but a *New Beginning*!

---

82   Thomas Jefferson: Letter to Archibald Stuart, 1791

Appendix: I

THE DECLARATION OF INDEPENDENCE

The Unanimous Declaration of the Thirteen United States of America

(Adopted by Congress on July 4, 1776)

When, in the course of human events, it becomes necessary for one people to dissolve the political bonds which have connected them with another, and to assume among the powers of the earth, the separate and equal station to which the laws of nature and of nature's God entitle them, a decent respect to the opinions of mankind requires that they should declare the causes which impel them to the separation.

We hold these truths to be self-evident, that all men are created equal, that they are endowed by their Creator with certain unalienable rights, that among these are life, liberty and the pursuit of happiness. That to secure these rights, governments are instituted among men, deriving their just powers from the consent of the governed. That whenever any form of government becomes destructive to these ends, it is the right of the people to alter or to abolish it, and to institute new government, laying its foundation on such principles and organizing its powers in such form, as to them shall seem most likely to effect their safety and happiness. Prudence, indeed, will dictate that governments long established should not be changed for light and transient causes; and accordingly all experience hath shown that mankind are more disposed to suffer, while evils are sufferable, than to right themselves by abolishing the forms to which they are accustomed. But when a long train of abuses and usurpations, pursuing invariably the same object evinces a design to reduce them under absolute despotism, it is their right, it is their duty, to throw off such government, and to provide new guards for their future security. —Such has been the patient sufferance of these colonies; and such is now the necessity which constrains them to alter their former systems of government. The history of the present King of Great Britain is a history of repeated injuries and usurpations, all having in direct object the establishment of an absolute tyranny over these states. To prove this, let facts be submitted to a candid world.

He has refused his assent to laws, the most wholesome and necessary for the public good.

He has forbidden his governors to pass laws of immediate and pressing importance, unless suspended in their operation till his assent should be obtained; and when so suspended, he has utterly neglected to attend to them.

He has refused to pass other laws for the accommodation of large districts of people, unless those people would relinquish the right of representation in the legislature, a right inestimable to them and formidable to tyrants only.

He has called together legislative bodies at places unusual, uncomfortable, and distant from the depository of their public records, for the sole purpose of fatiguing them into compliance with his measures.

He has dissolved representative houses repeatedly, for opposing with manly firmness his invasions on the rights of the people.

He has refused for a long time, after such dissolutions, to cause others to be elected; whereby the legislative powers, incapable of annihilation, have returned to the people at large for their exercise; the state remaining in the meantime exposed to all the dangers of invasion from without, and convulsions within.

He has endeavored to prevent the population of these states; for that purpose obstructing the laws for naturalization of foreigners; refusing to pass others to encourage their migration hither, and raising the conditions of new appropriations of lands.

He has obstructed the administration of justice, by refusing his assent to laws for establishing judiciary powers.

He has made judges dependent on his will alone, for the tenure of their offices, and the amount and payment of their salaries.

He has erected a multitude of new offices, and sent hither swarms of officers to harass our people, and eat out their substance.

He has kept among us, in times of peace, standing armies without the consent of our legislature.

He has affected to render the military independent of and superior to civil power.

He has combined with others to subject us to a jurisdiction foreign to our constitution, and unacknowledged by our laws; giving his assent to their acts of pretended legislation:

For quartering large bodies of armed troops among us:

For protecting them, by mock trial, from punishment for any murders which they should commit on the inhabitants of these states:

For cutting off our trade with all parts of the world:

For imposing taxes on us without our consent:

For depriving us in many cases, of the benefits of trial by jury:

For transporting us beyond seas to be tried for pretended offenses:

For abolishing the free system of English laws in a neighboring province, establishing therein an arbitrary government, and enlarging its boundaries so as to render it at once an example and fit instrument for introducing the same absolute rule in these colonies:

For taking away our charters, abolishing our most valuable laws, and altering fundamentally the forms of our governments:

For suspending our own legislatures, and declaring themselves invested with power to legislate for us in all cases whatsoever.

He has abdicated government here, by declaring us out of his protection and waging war against us.

He has plundered our seas, ravaged our coasts, burned our towns, and destroyed the lives of our people.

He is at this time transporting large armies of foreign mercenaries to complete the works of death, desolation and tyranny, already begun with circumstances of cruelty and perfidy scarcely paralleled in the most barbarous ages, and totally unworthy the head of a civilized nation.

He has constrained our fellow citizens taken captive on the high seas to bear arms against their country, to become the executioners of their friends and brethren, or to fall themselves by their hands.

He has excited domestic insurrections amongst us, and has endeavored to bring on the inhabitants of our frontiers, the merciless Indian savages, whose known rule of warfare, is undistinguished destruction of all ages, sexes and conditions.

In every stage of these oppressions we have petitioned for redress in the most humble terms: our repeated petitions have been answered only by repeated injury. A prince, whose character is thus marked by every act which may define a tyrant, ====is unfit to be the ruler of a free people.

Nor have we been wanting in attention to our British brethren. We have warned them from time to time of attempts by their legislature to extend an unwarrantable jurisdiction over us. We have reminded them of the circumstances of our emigration and settlement here. We have appealed to their native justice and magnanimity, and we have conjured them by the ties of our common kindred to disavow these usurpations, which, would inevitably interrupt our connections and correspondence. They too have been deaf to the voice of justice and of consanguinity. We must, therefore, acquiesce in the necessity, which denounces our separation, and hold them, as we hold the rest of mankind, enemies in war, in peace friends.

We, therefore, the representatives of the United States of America, in General Congress, assembled, appealing to the Supreme Judge of the world for the rectitude of our intentions, do, in the name, and by the authority of the good people of these colonies, solemnly publish and declare, that these united colonies are, and of right ought to be free and independent states; that they are absolved from all allegiance to the British Crown, and that all political connection between them and the state of Great Britain, is and ought to be totally dissolved; and that as free and independent states, they have full power to levy war, conclude peace, contract alliances, establish commerce, and to do all other acts and things which independent states may of right do. And for the support of this declaration, with a firm reliance on the protection of Divine Providence, we mutually pledge to each other our lives, our fortunes and our sacred honor.

SIGNATURES:

New Hampshire: Josiah Bartlett, William Whipple, Matthew Thornton

Massachusetts: John Hancock, Samual Adams, John Adams, Robert Treat Paine, Elbridge Gerry

Rhode Island: Stephen Hopkins, William Ellery

Connecticut: Roger Sherman, Samuel Huntington, William Williams, Oliver Wolcott

New York: William Floyd, Philip Livingston, Francis Lewis, Lewis Morris

New Jersey: Richard Stockton, John Witherspoon, Francis Hopkinson, John Hart, Abraham Clark

Pennsylvania: Robert Morris, Benjamin Rush, Benjamin Franklin, John Morton, George Clymer, James Smith, George Taylor, James Wilson, George Ross

Delaware: Caesar Rodney, George Read, Thomas McKean

Maryland: Samuel Chase, William Paca, Thomas Stone, Charles Carroll of Carrollton

Virginia: George Wythe, Richard Henry Lee, Thomas Jefferson, Benjamin Harrison, Thomas Nelson, Jr., Francis Lightfoot Lee, Carter Braxton

North Carolina: William Hooper, Joseph Hewes, John Penn

South Carolina: Edward Rutledge, Thomas Heyward, Jr., Thomas Lynch, Jr., Arthur Middleton

Georgia: Button Gwinnett, Lyman Hall, George Walton

Appendix: II

"Q & A"

I thought it would be a helpful companion for the material presented in *Blind Vision* to include a compilation of select questions, and my accompanying responses, as they occurred over a series of months beginning in mid-2008 including a few from as recently as March 2010. They appear in no particular order, and though I assure you none of these was scripted, I was pleased to discover a consistency in their resolution. I truly hope you will find them of interest.

1. **In your writings — by the way I really enjoyed reading *We Hold These Truths,* — and in your public comments, I often hear you use the word "perfecting." How can you really believe that humans can even be considered capable of being perfect?**

    Well, first of all let me explain how I use the word *perfect*. In most cases, I use the word as a verb as in; to per-*fect* a certain act, that is, to affect a "thing". Likewise, when I use the same word in a phrase such as: I am per-*fecting* the design of a building, I intend it to mean that I am engaged in the act of affecting a thing toward completion. In the use, as I often do, of the word in this context then it is quite conceivable, in fact, it is quite appropriate that humans consider the notion of working toward a more noble form as being consistent with man's higher calling. When engaged in the act of doing so, a perfecting, human, action occurs.

2.   You seem to be overly consumed with the subject of the government interfering with people's lives. I don't see how you can expect the government to do its job if it isn't able to pass laws that help people with their basic needs? It's the government's job!

Ok, I think I've got your questions and I'll attempt to respond to it this way: The moment one makes a demand on some thing, person or government there is also an implied understanding that this entity can both deliver on the demand and have the means to do so. But there is an even greater issue that must be addressed in this issue; the idea of permissible license or right. Do you possess the right to make such a claim upon this thing, person or government? Why is this important? Simple, the moment you make a claim or demand upon any of these entities is the moment those entities require a source from which to fulfill your demand which of course, creates yet another claim and this is were the problem begins. As with all things, their existence is the product of a source separate and apart from their own existence, animate or inanimate, and in the case with government, it has nothing to give but that it first doesn't obtain from somewhere or someone else. In the shortest most precise form I can think of and by drawing the point to a close; what you think of as the fulfillment of what you believe is the government's "job" (to help people with their basic needs) occurs by taking from one and giving to another and our Constitution makes no accommodation for this practice. The moment you license government to interpret what defines its job, you also must understand you release the influences required to perform it. Freedom is neither an imposition nor an executioner.

3.   Aren't there instances where the government should have the right to take what it needs to perform its job?

The nature of your question is so broadly expansive that I'll have to answer it with great caution, and in this way: Yes, but only as long as what constitutes its *job* is clearly defined and within the domain that considers *just cause*, and as long as it includes the narrowest of definition of what constitutes *public good*. Otherwise, in your example, if you leave government the expansive powers of self-determination then you also license the inevitable occurrence that it can define whatever it wants to whatever it wants. For example, if you leave what is defined as *the public good* up to interpretation, then it can mean that it is good for the public to have free housing, free health care, free roads, free food, free electricity, and so on. Is this not also public good? It is if that's what it is defined to be. What if the public good includes free housing, but in order to accomplish this you have to give up your home to provide the land for these free homes to be built upon? What if it is determined that it is for the public good that you should only eat once a day? Or that you should only be able to work at selective government work camps or watch only certain government-approved broadcasts? Is this what you have in mind? I certainly hope not.

4.   **What did you mean by "selective-governance?" It seems to me that you don't want to have government of any kind.**

Government has an appropriate place in daily life. After all, we do need some form of structure to manage the basic goings-on of contemporary societies that compose millions of people and their various practices. It makes sense, for example, in the case of transportation, you drive a car, I assume, yes? Ok then, consider what driving an automobile would be like if there were no code of conduct. Fine — if you are the only one with a car. However, if you populate the field with millions of auto-mobiles then of course you will have a problem. These are the perfect routines for government to regulate, that is, *to make regular, to normalize* but never to tell you whether you can own a car or how many cars you can own or their color, etc. The idea that I refer to as *selective-government* or similarly, *selective-indifference,* is the case where government is used by some vested interest to choose not only how government is applied but also the context and convenience to define it, despite your legitimate objections, as to what segment of the population is targeted by these practices and to what extent they are enforced. In short, some laws are passed to benefit a few, enrich some and dismiss those who remain. This is not representative government, this is government selectively applied.

5. **I enjoyed the interchange you had with the person who asked about your concepts of self-reliance, but I still believe that the rich should pay more in taxes to help pay for the huge costs of government. How do you justify your comments on excessive taxes?**

I have a question for you. Do you own a home? Yes, ok then, who in the audience doesn't own a home? Well then, a few folks down the row there, see the man? He raised his hand. Give him your home! It's yours, you say? Well, I'm the government representing all the folks who do not own a home and I just passed a law that requires you to give up your home. How's it feel now? You're native sense caused you to amass the means to afford a home and you set about the task of perfecting this ambitions. Yes? Ok then, this is self-reliance. Now, these so-called *huge costs* of government you speak of are the result of giving away free houses to folks who were told by politicians that these self-reliant rich people can be made to give you homes. Over generations they have been told that this is the role of government and now they know no other way and this is why you have perpetual growth in cost of government – in very simple and general terms. Now let's address the notion of *rich people*, quickly. I'm sure that if we take a census of incomes in this room inevitably there will be, among you, some with greater or lesser incomes than the medium. But it is also the case that every individual, but one, will have more income than he who is at the bottom – making all of you, but one, fall in to the category of *rich people*. Oh, I see, you mean the really rich, yes? The ones that have more money than anyone in this room. Oh, you mean those rich people, the ones out there! Do they know you're speaking for them? Keep your hands in your own pocket and don't worry about someone else's. I don't mean to be dismissive but my point is this: Government is very efficient at creating divisiveness by pointing to someone other than you as the cause for your lot in life. Yes, there are those who unjustly enrich themselves and I say, prosecute them. But to hold, as final arbiter, the vague notion of what constitutes too much based solely on the fact that you have less is not the sanctuary or domain of reason or justice. I'd rather see, instead, government act in a manner to promote an environment where you are free to succeed at the level you choose to fill your pockets with as much money as you please and not cultivate a climate of disintegration or contempt. Win at your own pace and at your own level and leave others to do the same.

6. **Ron Paul talks a great deal about restoring the gold standard to our monetary system. What are your thoughts?**

In principle, the idea is sound and relevant and I discus this topic in great detail in Volume II of the Blind Vision Series: *Value Given, Value Received* and as the topic is pretty broad, I will recommend that you pick up a copy of the book — you will enjoy it! But for now, let me just say this: As long as the global markets are as heavily manipulated as they are, establishing a uniform value for gold will be next to impossible — and due to the increasingly broad commercial uses of gold, it may likely be impractical. I do, however, believe that in the case of foreign trade, a nation's gold and silver bullion reserves are an excellent measure of national wealth and as a standard for trade. In other words, each nation's currency exchange, for global commerce only, would be based on a uniform global unit of gold/silver value. However, at the minimum, on the domestic level, the better standard would be to base a currency's value on the productive wealth of a nation and have its domestic currency volume float with that value. Note, I did not say base it on GDP, a completely false measure of economic output.

7. **Don't you think our monetary policy is directly responsible for the failure of our banking system?**

No, not at all. In fact, it is the banking system that drives our monetary policy. If you want to see true and effective economic change in this country then before you fix monetary policy, you have to fix the policy of banking. Politicians will never be able to do it. Many elected officials are attorneys and not schooled in understanding *dynamic-intervention*; they are schooled in the are of *selective-interpretation,* which is precisely why their methods have produced such complete failure. Not bad people mind you, just the wrong ones for the job. Legislation is not the process of practicing *selective-interpretation;* it is the art of perfecting and insuring supreme and ultimate freedom by assuring an environment where a free people are free to prosper.

8. **I'm having a very difficult time with your position on matters of social justice. It appears to me that you don't feel any sense of obligation to anyone. After all, collectively, aren't we our brothers' keepers?**

I can't tell you how delighted I am that you had the courage to offer-up this inquiry! Delighted, mostly, because this is one of the best topics for a really good discussion because it offers two very efficient examples illustrating how *relativism* appears in many inconspicuous ways. But first, let me address the middle part of your comment, something having to do with whether or not I feel a sense of obligation to anyone. Do I have it right? Of course, I feel an obligation to everyone, that is why you don't see me stealing your car or dumping my yard waste clippings into my neighbor's pool or spray-painting graffiti on the wall of a building that is the property of another. No my friend, others matter immensely to me. But somehow I don't think that's the answer you were looking for. That's what I thought. Yes, I do understand. What you mean is why am I opposed to accepting as my consequence the actions of another who prefers an environment where they can choose what defines that which becomes both the object of their choosing and the means with which it is placed at their feet? By the way, this is how I define what has become known as "social justice" – a universal application of unlimited scope and definition, selectively applied. Anyway, back on point: The answer is simply that in order to have what you suggest it requires a malleable form of right and wrong, a pliable sense of what constitutes justice and injustice and an equally unscrupulous interpretation of what it means to be free and what it means to be enslaved. I believe in the ideal that you should be free to give as you see fit and possess the liberty to object to the taking of something that you rightfully acquired by the product of your effort and industry, or that you possess by any lawful means. You can't make more of a thing simply through the illusion that by dividing it up somehow there is more — no more so than you can make something you have stolen yours simply by the act of taking it. Now, on the issue of the "brother's keeper" comment: Interesting particularly with reference to my last comment, but even more so on the issue of *misinformation.* Do any of you know the Biblical story of Cain and Abel? Quickly then; It is an allegory in the Bible recounting a lesson, arguably, on quality, giving, faith and hubris. Cain and Abel were brothers, the former a farmer, the later a shepherd. Each was called upon to give an offering to the Lord: Cain gave a lesser quality of produce from his field whereas Abel gave the first born of his flock. Upon finding that the Lord favored the offering given by Abel, Cain escorted Abel on a walk through the field and killed him. When asked, by the Lord, what had become of his brother, Cain replied, "Am I my brother's keeper?" Now then, within the context of its true meaning, it has rather curious overtones, doesn't it. The response, it would seem, is with direct reference to a *taking* is it not? The trite, flippant and indifferent response to the *taking of a life.* Substitute the word *property* for the word *life* and, well, sounds a little bit like government, now doesn't it?

9. **It's exciting to see Americans becoming active – you know, the Tea Party movement. I think it will be a force in changing the direction this country is headed in. Do you?**

I think the Tea Party movement is clearly a sign of the discontentment felt by most Americans. I also think that it can be a force, as you put it, for great change in this country, and more importantly, it can be a fabulous symbol for hope to people in other countries as well. I am however, hopeful that it will grow to a critical-mass phase – at this point, the government will be forced to respond. Now, and this is critical, it is in how the government responds that will be the area in which the people will need to be quite cautious. It must never grow violent, divisive or malignant; it must remain focused, deliberate and forthright, otherwise, you will witness first-hand just how far tyranny has progressed in the country. In the upcoming release, the final one of the Blind Vision Series, Volume III: *Valor in Prosperity*, I discuss many critical issues that deal directly with this, and a great many more, very much on this point — so I trust you all will be sure to obtain a copy. For now though, here are a few highlights: (1.) True and effective change must first start at the state and local levels. Without the states applying pressure, through both the legal and legislative process, the People will have a very difficult time effecting change at the federal level. (2.) Yes, the elected officials, at the federal level, have to be addressed however, without a specific declaration defining targeted issues around which the people, en masse, insist the movement will be easily fractured and redirected – much like the United We Stand/Ross Perot movement from back in the Bush/Clinton presidential election. Once this is established, then and only then will the People have both a barometer from which to assess viable candidates and a measure upon which performance can be mandated. (3.) Ultimately, the two-party system has to be disabled — and knowing that the existing structure will not self-correct, it will have to be overwhelmed, which will only occur by instituting a third party. We will have to use their tactics, the divide and conquer approach, if we expect to emerge from the chaos. And lastly, (4.) Do not be mislead, there are many systemic problems in this country and they've been accumulating for years and despite the appearance of formidability, each can be addressed and each can be resolved. Ultimately, I truly do believe that even our most profound difficulties and failures are ultimately survivable. This is the gift of grace.

10. I noticed you're always talking about the need to have a sense of something bigger than yourself, as if you think there really is a God or some master influence. I hear it in how you seem to disregard climate change but yet at the same time, well, I think you have a strange sort of reverence for things. I don't seem to be able to understand where you are coming from.

Next question? Anybody? Well judging from your expressions, looks like I'm going to have to try and deliver a cogent response, I'll do the best I know how. At the beginning of each of the Blind Vision Volumes there is a section titled *Series Preface*. Near the end of this section there is a story about a man who walks into a church — I suggest you read it, as it will provide some added context to what I'm about to say. With this thought in mind let me say that, yes, I do believe it is important to have, as you put it, a notion of something bigger than you but it's actually more than that. It is also having a notion that you are a part of something bigger and knowing that you are not only a part but that you are an integral part, so much so that without you, the whole is incomplete. Each human, each component of what exists is integral to completing the whole of what is created, to miss or omit but one is to lessen its form. Now, if you think of life in these terms then you must also think of what happens when you don't appear, when one abstains from participating as intended. Think of what would have *not* occurred had Jonas Salk *not* perfected the polio vaccine. Think of those who would *not* have survived and those that would *never* have been as a consequence. Oh yes, you matter, you matter immensely. With such precision, with such symmetry, and with such detail there simply has to be some higher form. It is all too precise, too kinetic and far too elegant to be mere coincidence. I have no idea what God is or even if God exists in such a way that can be defined in human terms, if at all – that is, to look like or resemble what we think of something comparatively such as in the case when we say "to look like a thing." Another way of saying this is, perhaps this: I've never seen anything in form or in function sufficient to establish a foundation such that I can begin to have even the remotest concept of what this God might look like or be. Heck, does anyone know what the universe looks like? But, I am absolutely certain that God is; the evidence, for me, is overwhelming. For me to think otherwise is to accept that no "thing" matters and thus, there is no value or purpose and that is something I simply cannot do. So yes, on these terms, I suppose I do have a sort of reverence, as you put it, but I also have a strong irreverence as well, which you've observed in my comments relating to global warming. Why? Probably because I see these as evidence of, shall we say, temperamental human vice, and as such, hypocritical, opportunistic and presumptuous. Hypocritical because it ignores the causal and functional forces, opportunistic largely because it's convenient and selectively interpreted and presumptuous primarily from the perspective that man believes his influence can both transcend causal forces simply by redefining and selectively interpreting how they apply. Man is extraordinarily powerful, but only to the extent that his power applies as intended by providential design. True, you may be able to move mountains but you can't make them - no matter how many "eco" stickers you place on your hybrid and absolutely regardless of what ex-U.S. vice presidents may write or say. In the end, they too turn to dust but what lasts, what transcends space, form and time, is the lasting impression your cause, as a human being, perfects the cause worth perfecting. Because you are human you matter and in order to matter in the manner and form your design intends, you must make what you cause appropriately matter as well! Why are you smiling? Don't answer, I know, when you put it this way, it's very difficult to object. As I realize, more and more the truth of it, I find myself smiling more and more too.

THE IMPERFECT
MESSENGER™
FOUNDATION
On Point • On Purpose • In Practice

Presents:

Blind Vision

Series

VOLUME I:

We Hold These Truths...

VOLUME II:

Value Given, Value Received

VOLUME III:

Valor in Prosperity

VISIT US AT:

www.theimperfectmessenger.com

FACEBOOK:

www.theimperfectmessenger.com/facebook

TWITTER:

imprfctmsngr

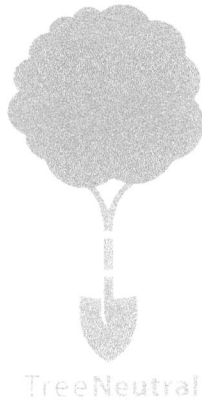

TreeNeutral

Advantage Media Group is proud to be a part of the Tree Neutral™ program. Tree Neutral offsets the number of trees consumed in the production and printing of this book by taking proactive steps such as planting trees in direct proportion to the number of trees used to print books. To learn more about Tree Neutral, please visit **www.treeneutral. com.** To learn more about Advantage Media Group's commitment to being a responsible steward of the environment, please visit **www. advantagefamily.com/green**

Valor in Prosperity is available in bulk quantities at special discounts for corporate, institutional, and educational purposes. To learn more about the special programs Advantage Media Group offers, please visit **www.KaizenUniversity.com** or call 1.866.775.1696.

Advantage Media Group is a leading publisher of business, motivation, and self-help authors. Do you have a manuscript or book idea that you would like to have considered for publication? Please visit **www.amgbook.com**

www.ingramcontent.com/pod-product-compliance
Lightning Source LLC
Chambersburg PA
CBHW022358280326

41935CB00007B/233